W9-ASF-838

0-8057-6947-1 $17.95

JOHN GALSWORTHY

Winner of the Nobel Prize for literature in 1932, John Galsworthy stands as one of the best-known and most influential British writers to come to prominence in the first decades of this century. In the enormously popular family epic *The Forsyte Saga*, Galsworthy presented a scrupulously accurate and meticulous depiction of upper-middle-class Edwardian life. In the character of Soames Forsyte, he created a vivid image of the British gentleman that still survives today. An immensely successful novelist, in his day Galsworthy was also widely known as a playwright and essayist.

Sanford Sternlicht's thoughtful study provides a comprehensive introduction to Galsworthy's life and work. Sternlicht begins with a balanced biography of the writer, and then moves on to evaluate all of his literary contributions. He places the novels, plays, short stories, and essays in clear relationship to each other, as well as locating them within the context of the English literature of the time. Sternlicht also elucidates the relationship between Galsworthy's brand of realistic prose and the reawakened interest in this mode among such mid-twentieth-century writers as Wain, Braine, and Amis. This volume is the first full-scale study of Galsworthy to incorporate his recent resurgence in popularity, inspired largely by the terrific success of the television dramatization of *The Forsyte Saga*. This renewed critical interest in Galsworthy has revealed him to be a writer not only eminently deserving of the success he enjoyed in his own lifetime, but also one of lasting impact on twentieth-century letters.

TEAS 447

JOHN GALSWORTHY
(1867–1933)
Photograph courtesy of the Mansell Collection

John Galsworthy

By Sanford Sternlicht

Syracuse University

CARNEGIE LIBRARY
LIVINGSTONE COLLEGE
SALISBURY, N. C. 28144

Livi......
SALISBURY, N. C. 28144

Twayne Publishers
A Division of G.K. Hall & Co. • Boston

John Galsworthy

Sanford Sternlicht

Copyright © 1987 by G.K. Hall & Co.
All Rights Reserved
Published by Twayne Publishers
A Division of G.K. Hall & Co.
70 Lincoln Street
Boston, Massachusetts 02111

Copyediting supervised by Lewis DeSimone
Book production by Janet Zietowski
Book design by Barbara Anderson

Typeset in 11 pt. Garamond
by P&M Typesetting, Inc., Waterbury, Connecticut

Printed on permanent/durable acid-free paper
and bound in the United States of America

Library of Congress Cataloging in Publication Data

Sternlicht, Sanford V.
  John Galsworthy.

  (Twayne's English authors series ; TEAS 447)
  Bibliography: p. 135
  Includes index.
  1. Galsworthy, John, 1867–1933—Criticism and
interpretation. I. Title. II. Series.
PR6013.A5Z75   1987   823'.912   86-31815
ISBN 0-8057-6947-1 (alk. paper)

823.912
G 178

to Beth

119770

Contents

About the Author

Sanford Sternlicht, professor emeritus of English and theatre at the State University of New York College of Oswego, now teaches English at Syracuse University. A wide-ranging scholar-writer-director, Professor Sternlicht is the author of the following books: *Gull's Way* (poetry), 1961; *Love in Pompeii* (poetry), 1967; *The Black Devil of the Bayous* (history with E. M. Jameson), 1970; *John Webster's Imagery and the Webster Canon* (literary criticism), 1972; *McKinley's Bulldog: The Battleship Oregon* (history), 1977; *John Masefield* (Twayne's English Authors Series), 1977; *C. S. Forester* (Twayne's English Authors Series), 1981; *U.S.F. Constellation: Yankee Racehorse* (history with E. M. Jameson), 1981; *Padraic Colum* (Twayne's English Authors Series), 1985; and (Editor) *The Selected Short Stories of Padraic Colum*, 1985. His many articles on subjects from Shakespeare to Graham Greene have appeared in *Renaissance Papers, Papers on Language and Literature, Minnesota Review, Harvard Magazine, Florida Review, College English, Ball State Forum, Midwest Quarterly, Calcutta Review, Studies in Humanities, Writers Digest, etc*. His poetry has appeared in over three hundred publications throughout the world, including the *New York Times*, the *New York Herald Tribune, Christian Science Monitor, Saturday Evening Post, Canadian Forum, Dalhousie Review*, and *Poetry Review* (London).

In 1960 Sanford Sternlicht received the *Writer Magazine* New Poets Award. The Poetry Society of America granted him a writing fellowship in 1965. The State University of New York Research Foundation awarded him fellowships and grants in 1963, 1964, 1965, 1969, and 1970. Sanford Sternlicht was Leverhulme Visiting Fellow at the University of York, England, 1965–66.

Preface

For the past sixty years millions of people around the world have considered John Galsworthy's depiction of Edwardian society as both authentic and current. After all, the author of *The Forsyte Saga* had received the Nobel Prize for literature and was highly esteemed not only by the British, but also by the leading European writers who had elected that quiet, gentle, courteous, reserved Englishman the first president of PEN, the international writers' organization. Although Galsworthy had pretty much restricted his view of British society to that part he knew best, indeed had been born into—the upper middle class—readers everywhere believed that the class values he approved of (such as respect for tradition, love of the countryside, fair play, support of the underdog, integrity in all human affairs including business, concern for justice, honorable behavior, comity between the sexes, and the code of the gentleman) and the class values he deplored (such as crass materialism, overpossessiveness, aloofness, indifference, snobbery, and phillistinism) permeated all of British society then and now.

In truth British society has changed greatly since Galsworthy's death in 1933, but the world's vision of the haughty, stoic, wealthy, tight-lipped, straight-backed, inarticulate pococurante, empire-loving Briton is still partly derived from the satire in Galsworthy's Edwardiana. Indeed, the British themselves, particularly the upper middle class, seem often to model their own behavior on the societal codes depicted by the most popular of the Edwardian writers. Furthermore, and curiously, the mores and manners of his characters have been both embraced by ex-colonial Anglophiles and parodied by Anglophobes everywhere. Thus Galsworthy's subtle influence lives on.

To study Galsworthy's work is to study the greatest English family epic, "The Forsyte Chronicles," which includes two trilogies and several stories; a series of engrossing novels satirizing upper-middle-class and upper-class British society before World War I; a body of plays by a passionate humanist and reformer whose international reputation in his lifetime was second only in the theater to that of his friend George Bernard Shaw; a group of finely crafted short stories, a few of which are still considered models for aspiring writers; and a collection of activist essays so effective in their delineation of the problems of the time that they helped improve prison conditions, the legal system, the rights of women, labor laws, the treatment of animals, and many other social problems. For John Galsworthy was one of the last writers, perhaps the very last, venerated for his wisdom as well as his artistry, whose voice was not only heard in the land but welcome and heeded in the corridors of power.

Galsworthy's reputation declined precipitously upon his death. The world changed rapidly in the 1930s with the Great Depression and the rise of totalitarianism, and Galsworthy's subjects and themes seemed less relevant. Now his star is beginning to rise once more. Although renewed interest in Galsworthy's biography began in the 1960s, this study is one of only two book-length, comprehensive treatments of Galsworthy's artistry undertaken since the early 1930s, the other being Alec Fréchet's *John Galsworthy: A Reassessment* (1969), first published in French.

Finally, the writing of this book was immeasurably aided by Mrs. Joanne Jones and by the interlibrary-loan staff of Syracuse University. I am also grateful to the English department of Syracuse University for allowing me the privilege of teaching the plays of John Galsworthy.

Sanford Sternlicht

Syracuse, New York

Chronology

1867 John Galsworthy born 14 August at Kingston Hill, Surrey. Son of John Galsworthy, a solicitor, company director, and property owner, and Blanche Bartleet Galsworthy.

1876 Enters Saugeen Preparatory School at Bournemouth.

1881 Enters Harrow.

1886 Enters New College, Oxford.

1889 Receives degree in law from Oxford.

1890 Called to the bar.

1891 Hunting trip across Canada. Meets Ada Pearson Cooper Galsworthy, his cousin Arthur's bride.

1892 Trip to Australia, the South Seas, and New Zealand.

1893 Meets Joseph Conrad, first mate of the sailing ship *Torrens,* in Adelaide Harbor.

1894 Business trip to Russia.

1895 Begins liaison with his cousin's wife, Ada.

1897 *From the Four Winds* (stories).

1898 *Jocelyn* (novel). Journey to Italy.

1900 *Villa Rubein* (novel). Meets Ford Madox (Hueffer) Ford and Edward Garnett.

1901 *A Man of Devon* (stories). Trip to Austria and Italy with Ada.

1902 Ada leaves her husband.

1904 Father dies. *The Island Pharisees* (novel).

1905 Trip to Italy and Austria with Ada. She is divorced. They marry in London on 23 September.

1906 *The Man of Property* (novel). *The Silver Box* produced at the Court Theatre, London.

1907 *The Country House* (novel). *Joy* produced at the Savoy Theatre, London.

1908 Buys house at Manaton.

1909   *Fraternity* (novel). *The Silver Box, Joy, Strife* (plays). *Strife* produced at the Duke of York's Theatre, London.

1910   *Justice* produced at the Duke of York's Theatre, London.

1911   Affair with the actress Margaret Morris. *The Patrician* (novel). *The Little Dream* produced in Manchester.

1912   *Moods, Songs, and Doggerels* (poetry); *The Inn of Tranquility* (essays). *The Pigeon* produced at the Royalty Theatre, London. *The Eldest Son* produced at the Kingsway Theatre, London. Galsworthys visit America.

1913   *The Fugitive* produced at the Royal Court Theatre, London. *The Dark Flower* (novel). Visit to Egypt.

1914   *The Mob* produced in Manchester.

1915   Mother dies. *The Freelands* (novel). *A Bit O' Love* produced at the Kingsway Theatre, London.

1916   Begins war service with Red Cross in France. *A Sheaf* (essays).

1917   Returns from France. Refuses knighthood. *Beyond* (novel). *Foundations* produced at the Royalty Theatre, London.

1918   *Five Tales* (stories). Examined for Army service but rejected as physically unfit. Galsworthys move into Grove Lodge, Hampstead.

1919   *Saint's Progress* (novel). Lecture tour of United States.

1920   *In Chancery* (novel); "Awakening" (story); *Tatterdemalion* (stories). *The Skin Game* produced at St. Martin's Theatre, London. Return visit to United States and Canada.

1921   *The Bells of Peace* (poetry). *To Let* (novel). First president of PEN, international writers' club. *A Family Man* produced at the Comedy Theatre, London.

1922   *The Forsyte Saga* (novel trilogy); *Loyalties* produced at St. Martin's Theatre, London. *Windows* produced at the Royal Court Theatre, London. Scandinavian lecture tour. LL.D. (hon.), St. Andrews University (Scotland).

1923   *Captures* (stories), *The Manaton Edition*.

1924   Journey to Africa. *The White Monkey* (novel). *The Forest* produced at St. Martin's Theatre, London. *Old English* also produced at St. Martin's.

1925   *Caravans* (stories). *The Show* produced at St. Martin's Theatre, London. Trip to America.

1926   Purchases Bury House. *Escape* produced at the Ambassador Theatre, London. Trip to Germany, Czechoslovakia, and Austria. Voyage to South Africa. *The Silver Spoon* (novel).

1927   *Two Forsyte Interludes* (stories); *Castles in Spain* (essays). D.Litt. (hon.), Manchester University.

1928   Voyage to Brazil. *Swan Song* (novel).

1929   *A Modern Comedy* (novel trilogy); *Plays*. Order of Merit. D.Litt. (hon.), Dublin University. *Exiled* produced at Wyndham's Theatre, London. *The Roof* produced at the Vaudeville Theatre, London.

1930   *On Forsyte 'Change* (stories); *Soames and the Flag* (story). Trip to Germany and Poland. Final visit to America. LL.D. (hon.), Cambridge University; D.Litt. (hon.), Sheffield University.

1931   *Maid in Waiting* (novel); *The Creation of Character in Literature* (criticism). Honorary member of the American Academy of Arts and Sciences. D.Litt. (hon.), Princeton University; D.Litt. (hon.), Oxford University.

1932   Nobel Prize for Literature. *Flowering Wilderness* (novel).

1933   Dies on 31 January at Grove Lodge, Hampstead. Ashes scattered on hill above Bury after dean refuses burial at Westminster Abbey. *Over the River* (novel) published posthumously.

1934   *End of the Chapter* (novel trilogy).

1935   *Collected Poems*, edited by Ada Galsworthy.

Chapter One
The Life of a Man of Property

John Galsworthy was born an upper-middle-class Englishman at a time when his nation ruled the seas and much of the world, and his class ran his nation. He had kind, generous, very rich parents; he was given the best education available to anyone; and he was an intelligent, handsome, healthy youth without much drive or ambition. He was never hungry for food or for fame. His class rather looked down their noses at achievement in the arts. Snobbery and inhibition were far more characteristic for them than outgoingness and creativity. Furthermore, he came late to writing. "That he wrote books that have a sure place in literature is a small, very English miracle. But then John Galsworthy was a very English man."[1]

Yet, when John Galsworthy died unexpectedly in January of 1933 at the age of sixty-five, no other living English writer, not D. H. Lawrence, nor H. G. Wells, nor E. M. Forster, nor Virginia Woolf, had the prestige, the power, and the public he had. Even his friend Joseph Conrad, who had predeceased him, had not had the success that Galsworthy enjoyed. His king had made him a member of the Order of Merit, the most prized award for English men of letters; moreover, he had been initiated into the pantheon of the world's great authors by the award of the Nobel Prize for Literature, only the fourth British writer to be so honored, and two of the previous three were Irish born. International writers had shown their esteem by electing him the first president of PEN, the organization for international authors, and he served in that capacity for nearly twelve years. In the eyes of the world John Galsworthy was *the* English writer.

In his most enduring work, *The Forsyte Saga* (1922), which was the first and only great English three-generation family epic, Galsworthy painted a portrait of his class. He limned his relatives into prototypes who show the current generation of English what their Victorian, Edwardian, and Georgian ancestors were like, and what their values were. Reversing Dorian Gray, the portrait he drew mellowed from satire to resigned acceptance to identification with the upper middle class as Galsworthy grew older and achieved recognition. Separately and distinctly, as a playwright he gave vent to his passion for reform, his acute sense of fairness, and his typically English concern for the underdog. Thus, to study Galsworthy is to study the changing soul of a people, as well as a literature in transition.

Great reputations sometimes go into a decline after a star is extinguished. In Galsworthy's case the decline was precipitous. At his death, Virginia Woolf, never appreciative of Galsworthy or his work, indicated in her diary that she was glad that "that stuffed shirt" had died, and within five years of his death he was almost totally ignored by critics. Yet popular readership of *The Forsyte Saga* in particular and of several of his short stories continued unabated from decade to decade, and his plays, although fading from the West End and Broadway, continued to be produced by innumerable repertory, university, school, and community companies in the provinces, in America, and in the dominions.

On 7 January 1967, BBC TV began to show the first episode of the twenty-six-hour serialization of "The Forsyte Chronicles." The corporation was so sure of the popular success of the material that it invested more money in the series than had ever been previously spent on a television production. Public reaction was enthusiastic beyond the wildest expectations. BBC reran the series in 1968, and subsequently over forty countries bought reproduction rights, including the United States and the Soviet Union. Untold millions have seen and loved the television epic, and the sale of Galsworthy's novels in Great Britain and North America reached levels far surpassing those achieved in his lifetime. New editions and translations have added to his readership.

Not surprisingly, the fresh popularity of Galsworthy's novels, sustained into the 1980s, was paralleled by renewed and favorable critical attention and a sweeping reconsideration of his significance as an English man of letters. A reputation has come nearly full circle; an artist's life becomes important once more.

Youth

In 1867 Victoria sat on the throne of the British Empire; Garibaldi began the march on Rome; Russia sold Alaska to the United States; Napoleon III withdrew his troops from Mexico under American pressure, leaving Maximilian to be executed; the British North America Act established the Dominion of Canada; Ibsen wrote *Peer Gynt;* and

Verdi composed *Don Carlos*. Europe had enjoyed a general peace since Wellington won at Waterloo in 1815, and "the sun never set on British soil."

On 14 August of that Victorian year a second child, but first son, was born to Blanche and John Galsworthy in their commodious villa on Kingston Hill, Surrey, only some ten miles from London. The infant was christened John as had been his father, his grandfather, and his great-grandfather. The Galsworthys would later have another son and another daughter.

The Galsworthys were a wealthy upper-middle-class family. John Galsworthy senior descended from old Devonshire yeoman stock. The family tree went back to an Edmund Galsworthy who died in Plymouth in 1598.[2] The author's grandfather was the first to settle in the environs of London, in 1833, where he lived prudently, invested carefully and well in real estate and houses, just like a Forsyte, and left his son a wealthy man. Galsworthy senior was set up as a solicitor and director of companies.[3] He was a conservative fellow, the model for Old Jolyon in *The Forsyte Saga,* and he waited until he was forty-five before he felt he was ready for marriage and a family. He married Blanche Bailey Bartleet, twenty-five, and of a good Worcestershire family of slightly higher social standing than the Galsworthys.

The author's father was an intelligent, well-read, handsome, bewhiskered, fastidious man. He read and enjoyed Milton and Byron and the novels of George Eliot. Later in his life he shared a love for the works of Turgenev with his son.[4] He was a fond, attentive father as many older fathers are. Galsworthy's younger sister, Mabel, remembered him as a man who was not a slave to work, certainly no "City Scrooge": "Head of a firm of solicitors in Old Jewry, he went regularly to the City every morning at eleven, returning every evening at five. The leisurely keeping of these unexacting hours left him ample time, in addition to his Saturdays and Sundays, for the enjoyment of his home-life, his gardens and his 'views' to his heart's content."[5]

Galsworthy's mother, a partial model for Mrs. Pendyce in *The Country House* (1907) and Frances Freeland in *The Freelands* (1915), was difficult, trivial, not particularly intelligent, and certainly not intellectual. Her entire world was her household, and she irritated her children by continually fussing with their clothes and hair when she saw them rather briefly at fixed hours during the day. Mabel says that "she was never very strong. I remember her as constantly on the sofa, a piece of Black Spanish lace over her head."[6] Of course she also ran a large Victorian household with a staff of fourteen. Nevertheless, she was not remembered with unreserved affection by her children, including son John.

The marriage was not a brilliant success. Husband and wife were both strong willed and uncompromising with each other. Fortunately, the many-roomed domiciles they inhabited and the conventional roles they played as breadwinner and household manager permitted much space between them. They could disagree yet manage to live together. Near the end of the senior Galsworthy's life, however, a bizarre incident broke the outward decorum of their lives.

When Galsworthy's father was nearly eighty-five, only two years prior to his death, Blanche accused the old man of making advances to one of the governesses of the grandchildren, and she left him. Unable to take care of himself alone, he spent his last days in the home of his daughter Lilian and her husband, the Bavarian-born painter Georg Sauter. As he lay dying, his son John sat by his side, day after day, reading from Dickens.[7] Blanche lived on eleven years after her husband died in 1904, traveling, making new friends, and thoroughly enjoying her old age. Of one thing she had been quite sure: "I don't want my son to be a famous author."[8]

All in all, the family in which Galsworthy grew up centered on a beloved, generous father who provided all comforts and much caring, and a diffracting, rigid, jealous mother. One Galsworthy biographer, Dudley Barker, points out that Galsworthy's unhappy parents not only had an obvious influence on his writing, but also affected his personal life. In that home life "it is not difficult to detect the first cause of the sense of guilt which deeply coloured at least the first half of his adult life, and which, aggravated by the social defiance of his own love affair, drove him to the five novels of protest, and in particular to *The Man of Property* [1906], and the creation of the Forsytes."[9]

The Galsworthy family lived in a succession of homes. First they moved out of London proper, shortly after Lillian's birth, to an adequate middle-class Victorian house at Parkfield on Kingston Hill. However, the senior Galsworthy soon bought land in the nearby village of Malden, known as Coombe, where he decided to build his establishment. He erected a huge Victorian Gothic jumble and named it Coombe Warren. It was to this house that the author was brought in 1868 a few months after birth. Coombe Warren was a tall, red-bricked, narrow-windowed piece of conspicuous consumption with a squat, spiked tower. It was, perhaps, the model for Soames Forsyte's Robin Hill.

The father built two additional houses on the land: Coombe Leigh, where the family moved in 1875, and Coombe Croft, where they moved in 1877. In 1881 they returned to Coombe Leigh, and in the same year, while John was entering Harrow, the family deserted the area entirely, having left a considerable mark on the land.

As an adult, John Galsworthy was very interested in his family genealogy, and he spent much time and money researching both his father's and his mother's lines. It was a part of his great pride in being an Englishman. In fact, about the only time he ever took angry notice of a reference to himself in a newspaper was when a correspondent referred to him as an Irishman. He saw his English roots as a source of his creative energy, as he indicated in a 1907 letter to his mentor, the critic Edward Garnett:

What queer mixtures we all are; and yet it's remarkable how, up to this century, class and locality kept themselves to themselves. Look at my origin for instance; as far as I can make out, my Dad's forebears were absolutely of the small farmer class for hundreds of years, and all from the same little corner of South Devon. And my mother's absolutely of the provincial Squire class. There's an old Worcestershire pedigree, Bartlet of Castle Morton, on her father's side too before Henry VIII, all marrying into the same class, quartering their arms, never distinguishing themselves; a tradition of course of coming in with the Conqueror. . . .

And it's queer how the two origins work out—how differently! The Bartlets have got a sort of crystallized, dried out, almost mummified energy; utterly unpractical, incapable of making or keeping money; narrow to a degree; restless; dogmatic. Long narrow faces and heads, perfectly regular features, lots of pluck; no real ability; no impersonal outlook; yet with a sort of inborn sense . . . of form.

The Galsworthys rising into the middle class for two generations with all its tenacity, and ability (of a sort), now seem in the third generation all abroad, as if melting away again into a more creative Sphere or nothing at all, muddling out as architects, writers, painters, engineers, do nothing at all, a non-practising barrister, a musicianly solicitor, one doctor, and a curious dandified land agent, alone represent the truly middle-class element and very poorly at that. What will become of them in the fourth generation? Very few have any children.

The one strain seems definite, clear, thin, and acid; the other all turbid, various, and unknown; I get I suppose any creative energy from the latter and a sense of form from the former.[10]

It certainly seems somewhat odd to an American reader that Galsworthy would consider his purely English background a "queer mix-
ture." It was, of course, his acute class awareness, much the subject
of his writing, that caused him to view the joining of a family stem-
ming from small farmers with country gentry as something remarkable.

Galsworthy etymologized his name, stating that it was derived
from the words *Gaul,* meaning "stranger," and *worthy,* a "fortified
homestead." As a result he changed the pronunciation of his name
from the one then current in Devon, the family's ancestral locale, and
generally accepted by all other Galsworthys, that with a short *a* as in
"gal," to "Gaulsworthy."[11]

Education

John Galsworthy received the best formal education money could
buy. In 1876, at the age of nine, he was sent away to Saugeen Preparatory School at Bournemouth. It was and is the custom for upper-
middle-class and upper-class boys, and now girls too, to be enrolled
in boarding schools often great distances from home. At Saugeen,
John—or Jack, as family and friends called him—was a normal and
typical pupil, bright, well behaved, and more interested in cricket
than in books, although at home he had been an avid reader of history
and adventure stories.[12] His acute nearsightedness, particularly in his
right eye, prevented him from excelling at cricket, although he maintained a lifelong love of playing and watching the game. He was a
fine runner, however.

In 1881 Galsworthy's father picked one of the great public (private)
secondary schools for his elder son to attend. At Harrow, John was a
good athlete, but only a fair scholar. His parents complained to him
that "if only he was not so weak in composition he might really dis-
tinguish himself at Harrow."[13] Bowing to inevitable peer pressure he
neglected academic subjects but became head of his house and even
captain of the school at soccer. His dress was affected, what an American today would describe as extreme preppy. In short, his appearance
and bearing reflected what he was: a wealthy, ambitionless, conventional, somewhat arrogant, but decent English public schoolboy. His
headmaster summed him up as "a quiet, modest, unassuming . . .
strictly honourable boy who made his mark both in word and play,
without affording any notable promise of his distinction in afterlife."[14]

It was either Oxford or Cambridge for him and father chose Oxford. So Jack went up to New College, Oxford, in the Michaelmas term of 1886 to read law. A contemporary at New College retained a distinct impression of the author at that time:

He came up from Harrow with a reputation as a runner and football [soccer] player; but having overstrained his heart at school, was unable to take part in athletics at the University. . . . [He] gave the impression of superiority. He was tall and slim, well-built and strikingly handsome; and always, I should say, the best dressed man in College. For the most part he associated with Etonians and Harrovians. . . . I imagine that he did not find his studies in Jurisprudence exciting. In any case he contented himself with Second Class Honours, being destined by his family for a career at the Bar. I think we all felt at the time that he was a very clever fellow with reserves of power, but no one would have predicted of him that he would be prominent as an imaginative writer.[15]

Galsworthy had convinced his chums and himself that he had strained his heart in school games. It was nonsense. His health was perfect. But the excuse allowed more time for being the dandy and parading his foppish clothes along High Street. Galsworthy never lost his interest in clothes. His lifelong appearance was as a wealthy man always properly dressed for the precise occasion. At this time too he adopted the monocle he used in public in his weak right eye, although he would wear eyeglasses working in private. He developed the habit of inserting the monocle and looking over a person to whom he was being introduced. This mannerism caused the false impression that he was cold and aloof, but in fact, he was merely straining to see.

Vacations found him at home, first in the luxury London flat his parents had moved to, and then to yet another house his father had built, this one near Regent's Park. The author made a study of horseracing and consequently was generally in debt. Also, during his Oxford years he fell in love with Sybil Carlisle, a girl he had met on a visit to Wales, whom his parents did not feel was suitable for their Jack because she was poor. It was a one-sided love affair, in any case. He loved her; she was merely fond of him. But it continued after Galsworthy received his degree in law from Oxford in 1889 and began his advanced law studies in London. On 29 April 1890 he was called to the bar as a member of Lincoln's Inn.

Galsworthy showed little interest in the life of a barrister, although he certainly was in a good position to make an excellent career. After

all, his father was a senior partner in a very successful firm of solicitors, quite able to throw many briefs his way. In fact, Galsworthy
never once presented a case to a judge. The one time he was supposed
to address a court, he was talking to his father outside the courtroom
and so one of his colleagues on the case made the appropriate applica-
tion. He did help his father in business, however. He wrote legal
opinions, and more importantly for his later career as a writer, he was
sent out to collect rents in slum properties held by his father's firms.
He saw the suffering of the poor at first hand, and the spark of the
reformer-to-be was kindled in him.

The senior Galsworthy was disappointed that he was unable to mo-
tivate his son, who may have been carrying a torch for Sybil, so he
packed him off to Canada ostensibly to investigate the affairs of a
mining company, but really to give him a change of scenery and a
chance to perk up.[16]

Shaping the Writer

At this time of his life Galsworthy met three people who would
have great influence on him personally and on his development as a
writer. The first provided an example of another kind of life. He was
the painter Georg Sauter, a year older than Galsworthy and a suitor
to the author's sister Lilian. He and Lilian fell in love while Georg
was painting the portrait of the senior Galsworthy. Of course, a for-
eign-born artist, even one with a fine reputation as a fashionable por-
traitist, was unacceptable to the Galsworthys. Nevertheless, the
couple slowly won over the family and were finally married in 1894.
Georg Sauter was a partial model for the artist Bosinney in *The Man
of Property*. Because of a second new acquaintance who married into
the family, one much more significant to his life and career, Galsworthy himself would also be a partial model for the tragic artist in his
masterpiece.

It was at a family party in 1891, celebrating her marriage to his
cousin Arthur Galsworthy, that John Galsworthy met the woman
who would dominate his life, although it was not until a second
meeting years later that their relationship would begin to form. Ada
Nemesis Pearson Cooper was the illegitimate daughter of Anna Pearson and the adopted child of a fashionable, somewhat eccentric obste-
trician, Dr. Emanuel Cooper of Norwich, a man who spent much of
the last of his lifetime building a giant Victorian mausoleum for himself and then sitting and contemplating it until his death.

Ada was born on 21 November 1864, but she and her mother concealed the true date of her birth, claiming 21 November 1866 as her birthdate so she could pass as the legitimate offspring of the doctor, although there is no evidence that he actually married Ada's mother.[17] Anna Pearson must have been terribly distraught to have given her child the middle name of Nemesis, the goddess of retribution, but retribution against whom? All that is certain about Ada's biological father is that he was not Dr. Cooper, although that gentleman left her a small fortune in his will.[18]

Anna Pearson took her children, now called Cooper, abroad upon Dr. Cooper's death. They traveled in Europe almost continuously from 1883 to 1889, either to find a husband for Ada or possibly to avoid doing so in order that Anna could maintain control of the Cooper legacy. Along the way, in the south of France, Ada met Galsworthy's first cousin, Arthur, a seemingly decent scion of a good family and a man destined to live off his father's money although he longed for a career in the army. The marriage would prove to be an excoriating one for Ada, and she would later either state or imply to John and his sisters that she endured beatings and marital rape.

Arthur Galsworthy would become the model for Soames Forsyte, the villain of *The Man of Property*. Yet other evidence from later sources seems to indicate that Arthur, although far from a cultured and intellectual person, was a decent, if dull, sort of chap, giving most of his attention and energy to a career as a reserve cavalry officer in the Essex Yeomanry. He served as an active duty officer in the Boer War, and although he was fifty-four years of age when the First World War broke out, he managed to obtain a commission and active duty again, serving in France until he had a stroke and was given a medical discharge. In peacetime he retained the rank he had earned in active service, that of major, and the family always referred to him as Major Galsworthy.[19]

While Ada was enduring her marriage, John was traveling half way around the world, and it was on these travels he met the third person who would greatly influence his career, if not his personal life. In 1892 his father encouraged him to take a long trip with a friend to Australia, New Zealand, and the South Seas. There had to be a practical Forsyte-like excuse for such a voyage of course, so the trip was undertaken in order that John could study maritime law problems in situ. In reality, Galsworthy's father realized that his son had little to do and no ambition for a legal career. John and his friend, Ted Sanderson, had fun and adventures in the South Seas. In March 1893 it was time to return home. They booked passage in Adelaide Harbor on a fast clippership, the *Torrens*. The first mate was a Polish-born sailor named Joseph Conrad.

At that time the unpublished Conrad was writing his first novel, *Almayer's Folly*. Galsworthy and Conrad became good friends on the fifty-six-day voyage. The older sailor spun yarn after yarn, many of which would become part of his literature. At the end of the voyage John was sent on yet another mine inspection, this time to Russia. Returning, he began to think of Conrad again, and in September of 1894 he wrote to Ted Sanderson's sister Monica, whose family was entertaining the sailor: "I do wish I had the gift of writing, I really think it is the nicest way of making money going, only it isn't really the writing so much as the thoughts that one wants."[20] Thus it seems apparent that it was contact with Conrad that gave Galsworthy the idea and the desire, if not the impetus, to write. That impetus would come from Ada.

Galsworthy's official biographer, H. V. Marrot, who wrote his book with Ada looking over his shoulder, states:

Ada Galsworthy's first marriage was a tragic mistake. Blameless and helpless, she was living in extreme unhappiness. Her two loyal friends [Lilian and Mabel] were doing all they could . . . and from them their brother began to learn—with what distress may be imagined—the torment that married misery can be. . . . There was as yet no thought of love between them; but he had always liked her, and now that his chivalry and compassion were aroused it was natural that she should become more prominent in his thoughts. So, gradually they grew closer.[21]

If Marrot perhaps was overstating Ada's marital misery, he most certainly was understating the impact her story had on the kind, generous nature of John Galsworthy. The theme of a beautiful woman trapped in an unbearable marriage with a cruel and unfeeling husband would provide an architectonic for a career as a novelist, and unhappy married women, based on Ada, would appear in novel after novel, from the lovely Irene in *The Man of Property* to Clare Corven in Galsworthy's last and posthumously published novel, *Over the River* (1933).

Ada was indeed a very beautiful woman at the time they met again in 1893 at the Eton-Harrow cricket match.[22] She had a classic profile, lovely brown eyes, and her figure was slender and stately. Her piano playing was exquisite. They began to meet often but always in the company of either Lilian or Mabel or both. She was twenty-six; John was twenty-three and quite inexperienced in the ways of the heart.

Then they met in Paris. It was planned. During Easter week of 1895 at the Gare Du Nord, Ada said some words to John that she, John, and most biographers and critics have noted as the start of John Galsworthy's career as writer. She opens her travel book, *Over the Hills and Far Away* (1937), with a description of the event. John "was remaining in Paris. I was traveling on under chaperonage. So behold us pacing up and down the busy, dingy, luggage infested platform, seeing visions and dreaming dreams, during which the fatal exhortation was made by me. . . . 'Why don't you *write*? You are just the person,' which gave the first impetus towards a literary calling to John Galsworthy."[23]

Obviously, Galsworthy had at least thought about writing previously, as indicated by his letter to Monica Sanderson, but clearly Ada wanted credit for starting John's career, thus implying, insouciantly, that a very great good came out of their illicit affair. Nevertheless, Galsworthy was deeply in love with her, and any suggestion she might make would have carried the weight of a chivalric command to a pining lover. It cannot be denied that her marital situation in those married-for-life Victorian times, her beauty, her love for him—and her courage in embarking on a shadowy relationship abhorred by the society of which they were very much a part—provided inspiration, subject, and theme for a lifetime of writing by a man who might never have written anything more creative than a letter to the editor of the *Times* if it had not been for Ada Cooper Galsworthy.

Indeed, Ada became a living part of his writing, before and after her divorce and their marriage. She continually encouraged him. She shielded him from everyday problems. She deflected the importunate. She lavished on him love and affection. She served as a sounding board for his ideas and first drafts. She typed manuscripts. She edited. She handled his appointments and correspondence. She was lover, wife, editor, household manager, and amanuensis.

On the other side of the ledger, she demanded unstinting, unrelenting adoration and attention from John. Her series of minor health problems, real and/or imaginary—asthma, rheumatism, continual bouts with colds or the flu—forced John to take her on annual winter trips to warm places around the world, so that another Galsworthy miracle is that he was able to write anything at all, let alone the volume he produced. He spoiled and pampered her. She needed this cosseting, perhaps to make up for the indifferent treatment Arthur had provided, or perhaps it was the surest way of tying her younger, handsome, wealthy, and growingly more successful husband to her for life. Not only did John not resist or chafe, he thrived on the relationship. They were themselves a great love story. Rightfully, he dedicated *The Forsyte Saga* to her, "without whose encouragement, sympathy, and criticism I could never have become even such a writer as I am."

Lovers

In September of 1895 John and Ada consummated their love. As the social world came to know of their relationship they were cut dead. R. H. Mottram, the novelist, a young protégé of Galsworthy, remembers being taken to the Junior Carlton Club by his mentor and seeing Galsworthy's handshake spurned by a fellow member.[24] Galsworthy resigned his club and the company directorships his father had arranged for him. It was imperative, however, to keep the affair from old John Galsworthy who still controlled Galsworthy's money and would have been shocked by scandal. The couple would wait ten years before they would live together.

Ada had left her husband's home while he was serving in the South African War and had rented an apartment in London. John had bachelor's digs nearby. John, the rentier, had little to do to occupy his time. Writing indeed was the answer. He had an adequate allowance from his father. He had one literary friend, Conrad, who was just beginning to receive notice. And he had the desire to learn this new trade. In imitation of Rudyard Kipling and Bret Harte he wrote a collection of short stories, *From the Four Winds* (1897), which he had published at his own expense using the pen name John Sinjohn (John, son of John). The book received some small but favorable attention, thanks in part to the groundwork done by the faithful Conrad, who in the beginning was overly generous to Galsworthy in criticism, and sometimes insincere, but who seemed to have sensed future greatness. Galsworthy grew into a writer worthy of Conrad's esteem. The praise came first, the reality later.

Conrad also began to introduce Galsworthy to important literary friends, such as the novelist Ford Madox (Hueffer) Ford, and he encouraged his younger friend to find a publisher willing to risk the expense of producing his first novel, *Jocelyn* (1898). Dedicated to Conrad, it is the story of a married man who falls in love with a beautiful girl whom he cannot have until his wife accidentally takes an overdose of medicine. The situation is somewhat the reverse of John and Ada's. The novel, derivative of Flaubert and de Maupassant, was not well received except by the loyal, if slightly duplicitous, Conrad, who wrote to a relative in Poland that "the book was not at all remarkable, but the author is good and kind."[25]

Better than his uncritical accolades were Conrad's introductions, and the most significant for Galsworthy was that to a critic willing and able to give him sincere, capable, and copious advice. That critic was Edward Garnett, whose wife was a translator of Turgenev. Galsworthy, painstakingly learning his craft, was modeling his next novel, *Villa Rubein* (1900), on Turgenev's style and technique, when Conrad brought him to Garnett's cottage in the summer of that year.[26]

Garnett was the reader for the publishers Duckworth and Company. English literature owes him an enormous debt, for it was Garnett, a writer whose own novels and plays are little regarded today, who as a reader and "improver" either discovered, helped, or promoted Joseph Conrad, John Galsworthy, Hilaire Belloc, W. H. Hudson, Arnold Bennett, and D. H. Lawrence.[27]

The Garnett-Galsworthy friendship and literary association, almost collaboration sometimes, lasted some twenty years, until Galsworthy felt more confident in his own judgment than in Garnett's, and the latter seemed to give up on the then famous writer who was past his peak and beyond his help.

Galsworthy returned to the short story form with the collection *A Man of Devon* (1901), which he dedicated to his father. In one of the stories, "The Salvation of Swithin Forsyte," Galsworthy introduced his great fictional family. He would not return to them for a few years, but the chronicles had in fact begun.

When the year 1904 began, Galsworthy's father was on his deathbed. The author now felt it safe to use his own name on his books. He had also developed enough confidence in his writing that he no longer felt that he might embarrass himself or his family by his work. The first book to bear his name was *The Island Pharisees* (1904), a novel in which a well-born hero encounters a romantically drawn tramp named Ferrand, who shows the hero the world of the poor and the hungry. In other words, Ferrand introduces reality and shakes up the bourgeois values of the protagonist.

Marriage

On 8 December 1904, after a long and harrowing sickness, old John Galsworthy died at eighty-seven, leaving his son a substantial legacy. Now at last Ada could obtain a divorce and she and John could legitimize their long, furtive relationship. They went publicly together to a farm called Wingstone, in Manaton, on the edge of Dartmoor, a happy place for them, which they had surreptitiously visited previously and which they would own later on. As expected, Arthur sent a private detective to observe, and Ada was served with divorce papers, citing John Galsworthy as corespondent. Then they left for Europe as soon as possible to wait out the divorce and the publicity. In two months Arthur was granted a divorce. Six months after the decree nisi, the divorce became absolute and the couple were free to marry, which they did in a quiet ceremony before the registrar at St. George's, Hanover Square, on 23 September 1905. Ada and John set up housekeeping as a "respectable married pair" in the small house on Addison Road in Kensington, which John had purchased in preparation for their life together.[28] Ebulliently, the mistress of ten years turned instantly into a housewife. Ironically, Ada, the single reason for which this least bohemian of writers left society, quickly led him back into its fold.

Alas, Ada never really recovered her self-esteem after the infinite number of slights she had endured as the writer's paramour. Like a child, she had to be indulged, petted, and always given in to. John had to inform guests that Ada was always to win at billiards. Her "poor health" required constant pampering and changes of climate. Concerned for his "dignity" as a growingly more important writer, she began to dissuade old friends, like R. H. Mottram, from addressing him as Jack. They had to learn to call him J. G. She did wait until after his death, however, to apply to the College of Heralds to design a coat of arms for John Galsworthy.[29]

John and Ada slept in separate rooms after the early years of their marriage. In the diary he kept from 1910 to 1918, Galsworthy cryptically recorded the times he and Ada made love. It was not very often. After 1912 those entries ceased. They had no children, ostensibly because of Ada's ill health. Dogs became the objects of deep affection. When their favorite of twelve years standing, the spaniel Chris, died in December 1911, Ada was prostrate. Chris had been their "child." Ada insisted that Chris's ghost came back to visit her at dinnertime twelve days after he died.[30] John wrote a biography of the dog, *Memories* (1914), a dog-lover's favorite read.

While John and Ada were abroad, waiting out the divorce, John was working on what would be considered his greatest single literary achievement, the novel *The Man of Property*. To say that Garnett helped shape the book is an enormous understatement. The men had previously discussed the plot while on a walking tour of Wales. Now Galsworthy posted sections of the novel to Garnett from Europe for criticism and approval. Garnett was generally approbative until he read that Galsworthy intended to have the architect Bosinney commit suicide when he learns that his lover, Irene, has been raped by her husband, Soames Forsyte.

Garnett really misunderstood Galsworthy's reason for Bosinney's suicide, thinking it was because the architect was despondent at having lost a financial law suit to Soames. He wrote: "I consider Bosinney's suicide an *artistic blot* of a very grave order, psychologically false, and seriously shaking the illusion of the whole story. . . . To make him commit suicide through money, is to make money paramount. But it isn't."[31]

Galsworthy was deeply hurt, but he was so dependent on Garnett's teaching that after explaining his motivation for Bosinney he rewrote the death scene. It was a compromise. Garnett wanted the lovers to run off together with her jewels. Galsworthy finaly wrote to Garnett, "Bosinney's death I think will gain in strength and credibility *as an accident* by judicious use of a suspicion of suicide which the reader by inferior knowledge is enabled to reject."[32] Never again, however, would Garnett have as much influence on Galsworthy's final product. But Galsworthy paid Garnett by dedicating *The Man of Property* to him.

Annus Mirabilis

H. V. Marrot called 1906 Galsworthy's annus mirabilis and indeed it was. That year *The Man of Property* was published and he emerged as a widely discussed dramatist with the production of his first completed play, *The Silver Box*. *The Man of Property* was not immediately recognized as the masterpiece it is. Although reviewers noted it favorably, none saw it as a contribution to the mainstream of the English novel, or realized that its memorable character, Soames, would become one of the immortals of English fiction, and that a term of

Galsworthy's, *Forsytism*, standing for anti-intellectual, antiartistic materialism, would be added to the lexicon. The public, too, was slow to take up the novel, with only about five thousand copies of the 1906 edition sold.[33]

However, *The Man of Property*, the story of the beautiful Irene, her unfortunate marriage to Soames Forsyte, and her ill-fated love affair with architect Bosinney, did place Galsworthy among the important novelists of the day: Henry James, Thomas Hardy, to whom Galsworthy dedicated *Beyond* (1917), W. H. Hudson, to whom Galsworthy dedicated *The Country House* (1907), H. G. Wells, Joseph Conrad, and Arnold Bennett. It was the theater, however, that propelled him into the public consciousness and conscience.

Thanks to the plays of George Bernard Shaw and the forward-looking theater managers Harley Granville Barker and John E. Vedrenne, the English stage was leaving behind the nineteenth-century traditions of the melodrama and "the well-made play" and adopting Henrik Ibsen's social drama. Galsworthy, with one well-crafted play after another, would add more natural dialogue and a less preachy format to the emerging theater of ideas.

The Silver Box, a courtroom drama of class injustice, which allowed Galsworthy to use his legal training, caught the attention of critics looking for a new dramatist who would write naturalistic plays of substance in the Ibsen, Strindberg, Hauptmann mode. Galsworthy filled the bill. Now he had a more immediate and direct outlet than fiction for his reformer's zeal. For twenty-three years he wrote thesis plays, most of them successfully produced in England and America, on such timely subjects as the labor-management struggle: *Strife* (1909); young men taking responsibility for the girls they make pregnant: *The Eldest Son* (1912); married women in extramarital affairs: *The Fugitive* (1913); the politics and morality of war: *The Mob* (1914); old money vs. new: *The Skin Game* (1920); anti-Semitism: *Loyalties* (1922); the harshness of the criminal justice system: *Escape* (1926), and several others.[34] Besides writing the plays, Galsworthy helped supervise almost every major production of his plays. He became, for the rehearsal run, a playwright-in-residence.

One play, *Justice* (1910), changed the system. Very few writers have ever done that. *Justice* is the story of a man who altered checks and is sent to prison. As was the custom of the time, he spends a long period in solitary confinement; that confinement and the generally unspeakable prison conditions destroy him. Galsworthy had visited the prisons at Lewes and Chelsford and had interviewed prisoners. He agonized over their suffering, and the cry from his heart became *Justice,* written in a mere six weeks. At the first performance, in 1910 at the Duke of York's Theatre, the audience refused to leave after the final curtain. They shouted for Galsworthy, who was not in the house. Until midnight they clamored, "We want Galsworthy!" The lights were turned off but they refused to disperse. Finally, Harley Granville Barker appeared on stage and managed to convince them that Galsworthy was not there. Slowly they left.

John Masefield, the poet laureate, called the play "an intense piece of truth [that] may have a great, perhaps an immense result upon our national attitude to crime."[35] Winston Churchill, home secretary in the cabinet, was deeply moved by the play. A correspondence between the playwright and the minister ensued. Galsworthy visited Churchill. They discussed prison conditions and strategies for change. Then Churchill introduced sweeping prison-reforms legislation that included reducing the maximum length of solitary confinement from three months to one. The minister wrote to Galsworthy that "there can be no question that your admirable play bore a most important part in creating the atmosphere of sympathy and interest which is so noticeable upon this subject at the present time."[36]

Before the First World War

In 1906 Galsworthy followed up the success of *The Man of Property* with a novel some of his contemporaries thought even better: *The Country House,* satirizing the landed gentry in somewhat the same way he had attacked the upper middle class in the previous work. Garnett said: "It's *splendid!*" Congratulations. I think *The Country House* is a great advance, artistically. . . . The writing is brilliant. You've quite surpassed yourself in many pages. . . . You have a great sense of the poetry of life coming in all the time."[37] Although not quite deserving of a place above *The Man of Property, The Country House* is probably Galsworthy's finest non-Forsyte effort in the novel.

Although he later learned to write anywhere, in hotel, on a train or ship, now Galsworthy needed to get away from London sometimes so he could concentrate more on his work and less on the public relations so concomitant with literary success. Although he would always keep a London residence, in 1908 he bought the farm house called Wingstone at Manaton on the edge of Dartmoor, in Devon, that Ada and he had visited before marriage and which John had come to love. Ada did not like its distance from the social whirl of London, its primitive lack of indoor plumbing and other amenities of modern life, and of course its dampness. Nevertheless, the years spent there before the First World War~were among the most productive of their marriage. Besides writing several of his best plays in the period, including *Strife* (1909), *Justice* (1910), *The Eldest Son* (1912), and *The Mob* (1914), he published three novels: *Fraternity* (1909), *The Patrician* (1911), and *The Dark Flower* (1913). A fourth novel, *The Freelands* (1915), was started in this prewar period, in 1913 to be exact. Galsworthy's first book of poetry, *Moods, Songs, and Doggerels* (1912), was yet another product of this fertile period. Galsworthy took his poetry very seriously and labored intensely over it. Critics, however, have generally given it short shrift.

One event marred what should have been the happiest period of the Galsworthys' lives. In 1910 Galsworthy met a beautiful, nineteen-year-old dancer named Margaret Morris at the Savoy Theatre in London during the post-opening night onstage party of a production of Christoph Von Gluck's *Orpheus and Euridice,* which she had choreographed and danced in.[38] They would fall in love and Galsworthy would have the one and only affair of his married life. He was forty-three at the time. Writing in her memoir of the affair, fifty-seven years later, in the centennial year of Galsworthy's birth, she recalled:

I was only nineteen, and John was old enough to be my father: so I was immensely flattered by his interest and the fact that he went on talking to me when he could so easily have moved away. He said the most wonderful things about the ballets I had arranged and about my own personal dancing, particularly in the Elysian Fields scene. I was still wearing my simple Greek tunic of thin cotton crepe, and he asked me: "But how did you arrive at such perfection and control of movement, which yet looks quite natural and effortless? Your friezes of figures were the Greek vases come to life, and it all looked so easy."[39]

At first Galsworthy's interests were professional and avuncular. He dutifully brought her to the house at 14 Addison Road to meet Ada, who seemed to take to the girl. He obtained a dancing role for her in his play *The Little Dream* (1911), and then the excellent speaking part of the cockney flower girl in his next play, *The Pigeon* (1912), even though she had had no professional acting experience. He pushed her in against the initial judgment of the producer. She received good notices, however, for both efforts.

Rehearsing with John on the production of *The Little Dream* for its opening in Manchester, Margaret fell in love with the handsome, well-known author. John, of course, was by nature kind, generous, courteous, and caring. One could call him chivalric in his relationships with the opposite sex. Also, he was no philanderer. Ada had been the only woman in his life since his early twenties. John made no advances at first, nor did he express any intimate sentiments for the younger dancer, who obviously adored him.

Back in London, they went into rehearsal with *The Pigeon*. Finally, things came out into the open:

It was horrible weather, and in the taxi back to the theatre John said, "You look terribly cold," and put his arm round me. That was too much—he had never touched me before. I snuggled up against him, and he suddenly said: "Look at me. . . . I must know, you must look at me." So I did, and he knew, and of course he kissed me and the whole world was transformed.[40]

For weeks they talked and planned to become lovers. But where? And how could they avoid hurting Ada? They would meet in her apartment, but at John's insistence, they sat at opposite ends of the room. Margaret naively believed that Ada would accept their love without jealousy after it was consummated.

Margaret stopped visiting the Addison Road residence. When John made weak excuses, the intuitive Ada broke down. Sometime early in 1912 John must have told Ada that he and Margaret were in love, but that his love for the younger woman in no way supplanted his love for her. Ada tried to be understanding, tried to avoid possessiveness. She wrote kindly to Margaret. But it was her "ill health" that came to her rescue. She began to fail, and soon John was sure that he could not have his love affair, with all its promise of inspiration and creative renewal, save at the cost of Ada's happiness, health, and even life. John decided to break it off before he and Margaret had even once made love.[41] He sent her a farewell letter asking her to be "a brave child." Although Margaret tried again and again to see John, and although they corresponded for a long time, they were never to meet even once more. Galsworthy tried unsuccessfully to get her some work with Shaw and Vedrenne, but she would never act on the London stage again. He sent her money for a dance school for children she had established, and he helped finance an ill-fated revival of *The Little Dream*. Finally, he gave her funds for an extended visit to Paris, where to John's relief she met her husband-to-be, the painter J. D. Fergusson.[42]

Galsworthy used this painful episode in his and Ada's life as material for the "Autumn" section of *The Dark Flower,* the novel which most closely parallels his own emotional life. The hero, Mark Lennan, like Galsworthy, has three loves in his life: the "Spring" love with his tutor's wife who sends him away to find someone of his own age; the "Summer" love with a married woman; and the "Autumn" love for a young girl which comes after many years of marriage.

The Galsworthys fled to Europe and Ada quickly began to recover. Returning to England for only two days to pack afresh, they escaped to America where Galsworthy's plays were having successful runs in New York. They traveled the width of the country by train, visiting the Grand Canyon, California, New Orleans, and Washington, D.C., and then sailed for home in May. It seems safe to say, however, that Ada never truly recovered psychologically from the shock of John's revelation. How could her knight in shining armor have betrayed her? She became even more dependent and demanding of total attention. Their sexual life ceased. John, who would live celibate for the rest of his days, suffered greatly as the final letters to Margaret Morris show. In July they went back to Europe, and on their return to London they decided to abandon the house in Addison Road with all its sad memories of Margaret and of the death of their dog, Chris. They moved to a flat in a house at 12 Adelphi Terrace, in which the J. M. Barries also had an apartment.

After moving, the Galsworthys took off again, this time to Egypt on a camel trip through the Western Desert. Oddly, Ada would later insist that they had "an incurable aversion from sightseeing."[43] Why the ceaseless peregrinations? Well, she believed it improved her health. Of course, it also kept John from developing other deep relationships, and it forced him to attend not only to the business of travel but also to her many needs. As for his compulsive need to create, she summed up her view thus: "Wherever we journeyed, that simple plant of the writer's profession, the capacious, well-furnished indestructable blotter, in friendly brown leather, went with us."[44] As for herself, Ada always brought along her portable rubber bath.[45] After John died, Ada never felt the need to travel again.

1914–1918

The First World War was a terrible time for John Galsworthy, as it was for everyone else in Europe. The England that this Edwardian writer had known and written about was effectively destroyed in the four-year bloodbath and the economic chaos that followed. Naturally, in 1914 he could not envision what a modern war would do to the humans involved. The Boer War (1899–1902) had pitted regular troops against farmers. Colonial wars produced few casualties, at least among the Europeans with their artillery and machine guns. The last large-scale war in Europe had been the Franco-Prussian War in 1870, and Britain had remained assiduously neutral. Galsworthy was a humanitarian who truly believed in the essential goodness of human beings, who hated the slaughter of animals, and who fought for animal rights as well as civil liberties. The slaughter and the loss of individual freedom in the First World War traumatized him. He wanted to help his beloved England, but at forty-seven he was too old to shoulder a rifle, and he was never sure, although the question tormented him during the period, if he could have left Ada to take up arms had he been younger and fitter.

The solution for despair was to write. Galsworthy decided that he would turn over all wartime-writing income to the war effort. As a result, his work in this period was often hastily executed and thus not up to his prewar standards. The money raised and donated, however, was quite substantial. Fortunately, *The Freelands* (1915), the last of his novels of social satire, was nearly completed by the time the war broke out in August 1914. His mother, however, was terminally ill at the time. Her suffering was much on his mind. He immortalized her as the model for the elderly Frances Freeland, the mother of four children including a novelist. Blanche Galsworthy died on 6 May 1915.

Beyond (1917), a story about a woman unhappily married to a Swedish violinist, was quickly done over the winter of 1914–15. Galsworthy himself declared that it was his worst written.[46] Essays, articles, sketches, and stories poured from the steel-nibbed dip pen he always used. *Five Tales* (1918), however, not only contains Galsworthy's finest short story, "The Apple Tree," but also his reintroduction of the Forsytes into his fiction with "Indian Summer of a Forsyte," as an epilogue to *The Man of Property*.

A second personal tragedy during the war, after the death of his mother, was the treatment his sister Lilian's husband, the painter Georg Sauter, received from the British government. He was interned as an enemy alien because he was German born, even though he had lived for most of his adult years in England and was beyond military age. Galsworthy petitioned the government for Sauter's release, wrote many letters, and personally called on cabinet ministers to no avail. After the war Sauter was repatriated to Germany and was left with such a hatred for England that he refused to return to his wife in London. Lilian's heart was broken and she died in 1924. Galsworthy's nephew Rudolph, whom all called Rudo, and who was a painter like his father, was first restricted to the vicinity of his home and then was also interned toward the end of the war, even though he was British born. After the war John and Ada would practically adopt Rudo as their son, partly to assuage the treatment his own country had afforded the youth.

The extended Galsworthy family, of which John was now the head, decided to give to the Red Cross the residence at 8 Cambridge Gate to be used as a club for the wounded, along with a sum of money to outfit it. While making the arrangements, Galsworthy ran into an old friend, Dorothy Allhusen, who suggested that John and Ada could join her in her hospital for French soldiers at Die, near Valence. John could learn to be a masseur and Ada could take charge of the linens. They agreed. It was something they could do and it did not conflict with the author's opposition to violence. John immediately began a course in Swedish massage and quickly became quite good at it. They crossed the channel to Le Havre on 13 September 1916.

John really had a gift for nursing. He had lovingly cared for Ada in all her illnesses for years. Ada was in top form, not only running the linen supply but also helping to entertain the soldiers, most of whom were suffering from nervous disorders and what was called shell shock in that war, and battle fatigue in the Second World War. Christmas 1916 found the Galsworthys well and happy doing useful, if somewhat amateurish, medical work.

They returned to England in March 1917. Galsworthy needed to start writing again. Also they wanted larger living accommodations; the Adelphi Terrace flat was no longer adequate. They went house hunting, and on 21 December 1917 they chose Grove Lodge in Hampstead, but would not be able to complete the move until September 1918.

At this time Galsworthy met D. H. Lawrence. The younger novelist had already published *Sons and Lovers* (1913) and *The Rainbow* (1915). They immediately formed an enduring dislike for each other.[47] Previously, Galsworthy had written to Garnett, "The body's never worth while, and the sooner Lawrence recognizes that the better."[48]

On New Year's Eve 1917 John Galsworthy was offered a knighthood by Lloyd George, the prime minister. John refused, feeling that such an award was not for a literary person and that accepting such an honor would be a betrayal of principles.

In the summer of 1918 Great Britain was running out of cannon fodder for the trenches, and even fifty-year-olds were being called up. Galsworthy had to report for a physical but was rejected as unfit for service. He was extremely nearsighted and had a bad shoulder from a riding accident. The author was embarrassed that he should be called in for possible conscription and relieved that he did not have to decide whether to serve or not. In the same month, July, at Wingstone, Galsworthy conceived the idea of making *The Man of Property* the first volume of a trilogy. It would become *The Forsyte Saga*. Galsworthy would recall that day, Sunday, 28 July 1918, as the happiest day of his writing life.[49]

Return to the Forsytes

The immediate postwar years found the Galsworthys traveling and John writing furiously again. *Saint's Progress* (1919), written during the last years of the war, came out while the author was writing the next group of Forsyte pieces: *In Chancery* (1920); the Forsyte interlude, "Awakening"; and *To Let* (1921). The reception by the public of *The Forsyte Saga* when it was published in one volume in 1922 astounded Galsworthy. Sales quickly topped one million in both Britain and America. The public had immediately sensed that he had written not only the history of their parents' generation but also the great national novel of their time, a work that captured the essence of something English, like *Pride and Prejudice, Tom Jones,* or *David Copperfield*. Moreover, *The Forsyte Saga* was quickly recognized as the great English three-generation family novel, the equivalent of Thomas Mann's German family epic, *Buddenbrooks* (1900), which coincidentally was first translated into English in 1924.

The overwhelming triumph of *The Forsyte Saga,* coupled with the critical and financial success of Galsworthy's latest play, *The Skin Game* (1920), propelled Galsworthy from his position as an important and recognized author into that of the preeminent living English writer. The last ten years of his life would find him writing prodigiously, traveling out of the country more than half the time, and reaping honors.

Travel in those last ten years was truly frenetic. It was as if the

Galsworthy's were running from something, perhaps trying to escape time itself. Journeys were made to Spain, Italy, Sicily, Tunisia, Algeria, Morocco, the United States twice, South Africa, Switzerland, Brazil, and Austria. Additionally, after Galsworthy was elected first president of PEN, the international writers' organization, he and Ada attended PEN congresses in Paris, Brussels, Berlin, Vienna, The Hague, Budapest, and Warsaw. Hermon Ould, a PEN colleague of Galsworthy, painted a cogent picture of the author at the beginning of Galsworthy's most illustrious period:

It was at the inaugural dinner of the PEN in October 1921 at the Florence Restaurant that I saw Galsworthy for the first time. I do not remember whether I was introduced to him. I can only conjure up a vision of an austere, courtly English gentleman, in appearance more like an ideal lawyer than an artist, whose hair was already grey though he was some years off sixty, and whose nobly domed head and steady steel-blue eyes did not encourage familiarity. I gained an impression then, later deepened and subsequently obliterated, that he was aloof, unapproachable, unbending. He was none of these things. He was shy, and for one so travelled and accustomed to ceremonies, peculiarly retiring, and his *sang froid,* I afterwards discovered, was quite fictitious.[50]

Other honors beside the PEN recognition began to accrue. The expected honorary degrees began to arrive: St. Andrews (Scotland) in 1922; Manchester in 1927, Dublin in 1929; Cambridge and Sheffield in 1930; and Princeton and his own Oxford in 1931. In 1929 Galsworthy finally accepted an honor from his king, The Order of Merit. Galsworthy felt that this recognition was more exclusive and more appropriate than a knighthood for a man of letters: Henry James had accepted it in 1916. The Galsworthys became celebrities. It is difficult now in these more cynical days to realize how deferentially world-class writers were treated in those halcyon days between the great wars. Newspaper people clamored for interviews, throngs gathered, and government and consulate officials met them at train stations and dockside to guide, wine, and dine them.

But Galsworthy was working much too hard. Plays were being produced almost annually, causes espoused, essays and stories written, and then he decided to expand *The Forsyte Saga* into "The Forsyte Chronicles" with the addition of another trilogy: *The White Monkey* (1924), *The Silver Spoon* (1926), and *Swan Song* (1928), in which he continues the story of Soames and his daughter, Fleur. He would show the literary world that the old Edwardian novelist could relate to and incisively satirize contemporary society. The trilogy was quickly republished in a single volume as *A Modern Comedy* (1929).

More and more charities, causes, and political groups made demands on his time, money, and writing skills. Once he listed the crusades for which he battled:

Abolition of the Censorship of Plays.
Sweated Industries.
Minimum wage.
Labour Unrest.
Labour Exchanges.
Women's Suffrage.
Ponies in Mines.
Divorce Law Reform.
Prison Reform: (Closed Cell Confinement).
Aeroplanes in War.
Docking of Horses' Tails.
For Love of Beasts.
Slaughterhouse Reform.
Plumage Bill.
Caging of Wild Birds.
Worn-out Horse Traffic.
Performing Animals.
Vivisection of Dogs.
Pigeon Shooting.
Slum Clearance.
Zoos.
Cecil Houses.
Children on the Stage.
The Three-Year Average Income Tax.[51]

On top of everything else pending in his life, Galsworthy also decided to move. Rudolph Sauter and his wife, Viola, had become a part of the Galsworthy household and traveling entourage. John now felt that Wingstone and Grove Lodge were not large enough for the four of them, his work, and Rudo's painting. Although he first wanted a small country house, in 1926 to the dismay of the Sauters, who were going to have to run the establishment, he bought a house that Soames Forsyte and John Galsworthy Senior would have admired: Bury House, halfway between Pulborough and Arundel in Sussex, with a view of Bury Hill. It was a Tudor-style mansion containing twenty-two rooms, fifteen of which were bedrooms, and it dictated a grand style of life which hitherto Galsworthy had avoided. Additionally, Grove Lodge was retained as the London town house.

Galsworthy still could not depart from the Forsytes even though he had killed off Soames in *Swan Song*. More Forsyte tales appeared in *On Forsyte 'Change* (1930). Galsworthy also embarked on a third trilogy, the story of the Charwell family, an older, more traditional clan than the Forsytes. Again he was working constantly, as if against a clock. The first Charwell book, *Maid in Waiting,* appeared in 1931, followed the next year by *Flowering Wilderness*. Exhausted, he completed *Over the River* on 13 August 1932, the day before his sixty-fifth birthday. It would be published posthumously the next year. Galsworthy's cousin and goddaughter, Dorothy Easton, saw him at a PEN dinner at that time. She noted that "he looked paler, laced in and rather like a lion in a cage."[52]

The Prize and Death

While writing *Over the River* Galsworthy was depressed. A slightly disfiguring growth on his nose, which had piqued his vanity, had been cured by radium treatments. He had had some falls from his horse. Most disquieting to him and his friends was that he had suffered attacks of stuttering so severe that he would temporarily lose the power of speech. Ada seemed not to notice her husband's rapid decline although it was frighteningly clear to Rudo, who saw his uncle begin to drag one leg slightly. Galsworthy refused medical aid. It was as if he knew that he was dying and he wanted to keep it from Ada for as long as possible.

On 10 November 1932 the announcement arrived from Stockholm that John Galsworthy had won the Nobel Prize for Literature. The news rallied Galsworthy as he and Ada prepared for yet another trip, this time to Stockholm to receive the award. Galsworthy prepared a speech but was unable to rehearse it without stumbling and stuttering. It was then he realized that the trip was impossible. Rudo wrote to Stockholm that Galsworthy would be unable to attend the awards ceremony. Finally a visit to a London specialist, but it proved inconclusive. Ada now took notice and became panic-stricken as the decline continued. How could she live without John? They took him to Grove Lodge. Belatedly, medical authorities began to suspect a brain tumor. The symptoms were all there, including the severe headaches he had concealed.

The Nobel Prize medal was delivered to Grove Lodge. King George V sent for news. The prime minister phoned. The world waited. On the morning of 31 January 1933, after a final struggle, John Galsworthy died. He was sixty-five years old. His body was privately cremated on 3 February.

John Galsworthy was not a religious observant. He was not married in a church nor buried in consecrated ground, but in his writing he strove to know God through the ways of humanity.[53] A grand memorial service attended by the nation's notables was held in Westminster Abbey, although permission for Abbey burial was refused by the dean, Dr. Foxley Norris. Galsworthy had written a poem on a sheet of paper instructing: "Scatter my ashes! / . . . Mingle my dust with the dust, / Give me in fee to the wind!"[54] On 25 March 1933 Rudo scattered his ashes on Bury Hill. Ada lived on twenty-three years in a relatively healthy old age. Upon her death she too was cremated and her ashes scattered on Bury Hill.

Chapter Two
The Gentleman Writer: Early Novels

It is because most of Galsworthy's early novels are works of social criticism that he was given the sobriquet Edwardian novelist. Today that is a descriptive term; it was once derisive. In 1924 in her oft-cited essay "Mr. Bennett and Mrs. Brown," Virginia Woolf, so different a novelist from Galsworthy with her emphasis on introspection into individual human experience, specified 1910 as the dividing line between the Edwardian and Georgian novel. The Edwardians were Galsworthy, H. G. Wells, and Arnold Bennett; the Georgians included E. M. Forster, D. H. Lawrence, and James Joyce. Referring to the former she says, "To go to these men and ask them to teach you how to write a novel—how to create characters that are real—is precisely like going to a bootmaker and asking him to teach you how to make a watch."[1] In other words, they were craftsmen who did not know their craft. Woolf continues her attack saying: "The Edwardians were never interested in character in itself; or in the book itself. They were interested in something outside."[2]

Virginia Woolf was writing across a great gulf, not of time but of events. The First World War had forever altered English society, and if much of what she had to say about that older generation of writers is acerbic, it is true that unlike herself, and perhaps Joyce too, the Edwardians were deeply interested in the world beyond art, for after the debacle of Oscar Wilde they had come to reject Walter Pater and the concept of art for art's sake, while accepting Max Nordau's view in *Degeneration* (English edition 1895) that the race was degenerating spiritually and physically.

Thus the Edwardians addressed themselves to the problems and the questions of their day: the epistemological crisis resulting from the slow Victorian drift away from God and toward Darwinism; the loss of moral certitude and imperial conviction in the aftermath of the Boer War (1899–1902); and the concern for, and the fear of, the increasingly alienated and dispossessed working class. The England then in which Galsworthy matured as a writer and which became his all-pervasive subject was, as John Batchelor recently concluded, "a relatively stable and yet uneasy culture in which 'odours from the abyss' reminded the upper classes of a level of poverty and 'degeneracy' which they preferred not to acknowledge . . . a culture in which the great Victorian imperatives, Christianity, Monarchy, Empire, had largely been replaced by secular consolations which for some writers were still current—rural England, adventures in action, social ascendancy."[3]

First Efforts

John Galsworthy trained for the law, dabbed into business, and drifted into writing. He began as a twenty-seven-year-old dilettante, slowly working on stories when, as was often the case, there was nothing else to do in his tiny law office at 3 Paper Buildings in the Temple.[4] Quite naturally, he emulated those writers he admired: Guy de Maupassant, Rudyard Kipling, Bret Harte, and Ivan Turgenev. His self-disciplined apprenticeship was a six-year one in which he produced four books under the pseudonym John Sinjohn. The first and the fourth are collections of stories: *From the Four Winds* (1897) and *A Man of Devon* (1901). They are discussed in chapter 6. The second and the third are novels.

Jocelyn (1898) embarrassed Galsworthy later in life. He never allowed a reprint in his lifetime, ostensibly because it was "a poor thing." Looking at the novel now one sees that even more than *The Man of Property* it is the barely masked story of John and Ada. There has been renewed interest in the book, reprinted in 1976, because it introduces the two modes of Galsworthy's pre–World War I work: social criticism and romance, and it foreshadows the skill as a storyteller he would develop later in that period.

Galsworthy's first novel is a psychological study and a love story. Giles Legard, the first of several Galsworthy heroes who are well-to-do and without an occupation, is a thirty-five-year-old Englishman living abroad with a wife who is dying of consumption. He falls in love with a beautiful but frigid English girl named Jocelyn Ley: "A delicate oval face, cold as the moonlight itself; averted with unseizable eyes, profound and dark, with the lids drooping over them . . . lips drawn together, cruelly set; cheeks colourless; between the brows a slight furrow; and over all the waving dark hair gathered back from the low forehead."[5] Jocelyn causes Giles great suffering when she refuses sex with him. Finally they become lovers, but Jocelyn is in despair because she is also friends with Giles's wife, Irma, who becomes aware of her husband's feelings for her friend and takes an overdose of morphine, which leaves her in a coma but still alive. Giles finds her but leaves her to her fate and proceeds to a previously arranged meeting with his lover. Irma dies and the lovers feel responsibility and guilt. Believing that their love will forever be overshadowed by Irma's death, they separate, but finally reunite in England.

Although *Jocelyn* is primarily a romantic novel, it also satirizes and criticizes the deracinated upper-class English who live for play, in such watering holes as Monte Carlo, and thus in a sense never grow beyond childhood. The novel is tense and somewhat obscure because the author has not as yet mastered his prose and is overwriting. However, its youthful frankness and willingness to deal directly with sexual passion and frustration give it a sense of modernity missing in most other novels written at that time and cause one to remember that Galsworthy's career as a novelist commenced at the same time that Sigmund Freud began publishing his major theories.

Lastly, *Jocelyn* introduces the first of a parade of brilliantly portrayed older women and men who would become a hallmark of his fiction. Mrs. Tavis, perhaps modeled on Ada's mother, is Jocelyn's aunt and traveling companion. She is neither very bright nor very devoted to her chaperonage. Sharply observant of her type, Galsworthy endows the character with a memorable comic philistinism.

Galsworthy's second novel, *Villa Rubein* (1900), marked an advance for the writer. He himself believed he had turned a corner with this work and had begun to master the primary technique of fiction.[6] Ford Madox (Hueffer) Ford felt it had the essential quality of distinction.[7] Based on his sister Lilian's love for, and subsequent marriage to, the painter Georg Sauter, it is the story of a young Austrian painter, Alois Harz, and his love for an English girl of gentle and noble character, Christian Devorell. It is set in the Villa Rubein at Botzen (Bolzano), in the Austrian Alps. Her family disapproves and her Czech stepfather, having learned that Harz, years earlier, had escaped from police arrest as a student anarchist, informs on him. Christian's English uncle, Nicholas Treffry, helps her lover escape by taking the young man on a perilous and physically exhausting journey to safety over the Alps and across the Italian border. This effort brings on a fatal illness in the uncle, which parts the lovers. There is, however, a happy, if gratuitous, ending with the lovers winding up as husband and wife in London.

In *Villa Rubein* Galsworthy first begins to depict the London businessmen of whom the Forsytes are the epitome. In fact, it is in this novel that we first hear the name Forsyte, for the old heroic uncle is a partner in the firm of "Forsyte and Treffry, teamen, of the Strand."[8] Perhaps the finest characterization in this novel is that of Treffry, the upper-middle-class type of Victorian gentleman whom Galsworthy knew and understood so well. Treffry is the antecedent for the upright old Forsyte men: Jolyon, James, and Swithin. Nevertheless, *Villa Rubein* is a slighter effort than is *Jocelyn*. It is less of a love story and hardly satirical. Galsworthy, however, is getting better with natural description, and he has hit on the idea of using an English family in conflict—in this case battling over the question of art vs. society's pressure—as the central psychological background and resource for a novel.

The Novels of Social Criticism

The Island Pharisees (1904), *The Country House* (1907), *Fraternity* (1909), *The Patrician* (1911), and *The Freelands* (1915), along with the masterpiece *The Man of Property* (1906), the keystone of *The Forsyte Saga* to be discussed in chapter 3, form the core of the body of work that raised Galsworthy to literary prominence and caused him to be linked with Wells and Bennett as one of the three most significant Edwardian novelists who chose their own people as material for social commentary and satire. These writers examined the conflict between self and culture. In their novels, society takes the place of God or the gods in determining what is good and what is evil. Society becomes the creator and arbiter of values.[9]

Galsworthy's novels of social criticism introduce the main themes of his fiction, themes to which he would remain loyal through his last work: the hero as gentleman, one whose actions are circumscribed by class restrictions even as he struggles to surmount these restrictions; the struggle both in society and within specific characters between natural driving forces, such as instinct, and such manifestations of the superego as principle, idealism, and duty; the concept that one's character is one's destiny and although society struggles mightily to determine character, it finally emerges from individual qualities; art and philistinism locked in mortal combat; and passion and marriage as both antithetical and antagonistic. The last theme is the predominant one in Galsworthy's fiction.

The first of the socially engaged novels of Galsworthy, *The Island*

Pharisees, is also the first novel he published under his own name. It is a bildungsroman like Samuel Butler's *The Way of All Flesh* (1903), a contemporary novel Galsworthy much admired, James Joyce's *A Portrait of the Artist as a Young Man* (1917), and D. H. Lawrence's *Sons and Lovers* (1913), dealing with the maturation and growing social awareness of a young man. Two characters dominate the novel: Richard Shelton, the naive, affluent English hero, and his countercheck, a young Flemish tramp named Ferrand, through whom Galsworthy lays open the hypocrisy and blatant materialism of the "island pharisees," that is, the English. Ferrand will appear again and again in Galsworthy's work, in his short stories and in the play *The Pigeon* (1912). He is based on a person named Clermont, whom Galsworthy met years before in Paris.

Galsworthy, so dependent on his father's wealth and not sure if he ever could survive on his own, was fascinated by a personality that had the talent, experience, courage, and independence to survive and remain free of society's dictates. In his Nobel speech Galsworthy spoke of meeting Clermont when he "breakfasted off bread and the good water of fountains."[10] Clermont, whose letters Galsworthy treasured all his life, wrote, "Verily I say unto you it is harder for one of the black-coated fraternity to enter the world of the disinherited than for a camel to pass through the eye of a needle."[11] Galsworthy then admitted, "It has been too hard for me."[12]

Borrowing from Turgenev's novel *Rudin* (1856), a story of a broken engagement, which he admired, Galsworthy tells the history of Shelton's engagement to Antonia Dennant, a girl of his class.[13] On his way home from France Shelton is sympathetic to two foreigners in an English third-class train compartment; one is a pregnant French girl and the other is Ferrand, who is trying to help the woman while the complacent English shun her. When he and Shelton strike up a friendship, Ferrand comments: "Haven't you observed . . . that those who by temperament and circumstance are worst fitted to pronounce judgement are usually the first to judge? The judgements of society are always childish, seeing that it's composed for the most part of individuals who have never smelt the fire. . . . They who have money run too great a risk of parting with it if they don't accuse the penniless of being rogues and imbeciles."[14]

Ferrand functions as Shelton's (and Galsworthy's) alter ego. He expresses the social criticism that the young, upper-middle-class Englishman has sometimes felt but has found difficult to express because of his upbringing and his fear of class disapproval: "Shelton was startled, and not only by an outburst of philosophy from an utter stranger in poor clothes, but at this singular wording of his own private thoughts" (*IP*, 9).

As his sensibilities develop, Shelton comes to see his family and friends in a new light. Their pharisaical existence is more shallow and meaningless than that of the struggling and improvident masses. The young man enters into the world of the slum and the doss house. His conscience sours as he realizes: "I am a Pharisee, like all the rest who aren't in the pit. My respectability is only luck" (*IP*, 34).

Proceeding on his disenchanted journey, he soon leaves behind the poor—with whom neither Shelton nor Galsworthy were ever comfortable for long—to judge his own class with severity:

Their talk, like that of many dozens of fine couples invading London from their country places, was of where to dine, what theatre they should go to, whom they had seen, what they should buy. And Shelton knew that from day's end to end, and even in their bed, these would be the subjects of their conversation. They were the best-bred people of the sort he met in country houses and accepted as of course, with a vague discomfort at the bottom of his soul. . . . They were the best-bred people of the sort who supported charities, knew everybody, had clear, calm judgement, and intolerance of all such conduct as seemed to them "impossible," all breaches of morality, such as mistakes of etiquette, such as dishonesty, passion, sympathy (except with a canonized class of objects—the *legitimate* sufferings, for instance, of their own families and class). (*IP*, 35)

Even at Oxford, where Shelton hopes to find enlightenment, he sees provinciality, lack of compassion, and moral stagnation. Shelton himself proves to be a moral coward when he refuses to help a prostitute because it might endanger his position with Antonia.

Through his portrait of Shelton's fiancée, Galsworthy comes down hard on the women of his class and time. Antonia has all the necessary equipment for Edwardian seduction: good looks, self-assuredness, the ability to tantalize men sexually and then to dart into the armor of chastity and propriety. Shelton comes to realize how artificial this kind of woman is, when Antonia, because she is uncomfortable with, and frightened of, Ferrand, is antagonistic toward the poor philosopher. Finally, as generous impulse overcomes mean respectability, Shelton does something bold and courageous. He helps a woman who, like Ada, is a victim of an unhappy marriage. Offended, Antonia breaks off the engagement, then rescinds her decision; but it is too late. With eyes opened and sensibilities sharpened, Shelton refuses her and experiences "a feeling of relief, like one who drops exhausted at his journey's end" (*IP*, 317).

In *The Island Pharisees* Galsworthy finds his own voice as a novelist. The book is serious of purpose as it accurately depicts the frustration, disillusionment, confusion, and most significantly, the social awareness developing in the scions of the English middle class in the transitional years between the Boer War and the First World War, between Victorianism and "modern times."

The weaknesses of *The Island Pharisees* are the amorphousness of the social criticism, Galsworthy's stilting self-consciousness as a writer, and the slight and unresolved plot. Shelton has not solved any of his problems except that of his misguided engagement, nor does he have a plan of action for the future. Still the book was favorably reviewed and deservedly praised as a revolutionary work. Galsworthy had questioned the values of the establishment. It was not often done. The conservative Edwardian world saw Galsworthy now as a radical writer and reformer.[15]

The success of *The Man of Property* was followed by the equally successful *The Country House*. Edward Garnett called *The Country House* "the finest of all his novels."[16] In *The Country House* "Galsworthy . . . explores the pathos of the culturally obsolete."[17] Now the naturalist, the author dissects, with both touches of cruelty and nostalgia, the fading of the narrow, prejudiced, and hypocritical world of both his and the Forsyte's country cousins. And once again the novel centers on a love affair between a young man and an unhappily married woman; as in *The Man of Property* and elsewhere, the pervasive theme of the irreconcilability of passion and marriage is the author's wealth and poverty as a novelist. In fact, Galsworthy started the novel under the title "Danae," and it was to be a psychological study of a vivacious woman unburdened by a moral sense, but in beginning over he returned to the passion vs. marriage theme.

Essentially, *The Country House* deals with the landed gentry in the way *The Man of Property* deals with the moneyed bourgeoisie; it treats them as a subculture in crisis. The Pendyce family are feudal rulers of their land and the agriculturalists who work for them. They are entrenched in their ancient ways of privilege, refusing to change with the times. Their rigid taboos deprive them of generous instincts and access to both the beauty and the pain in the great world beyond their ghetto of comfort and advantage. Thus they suffer from what Galsworthy calls "Pendycitis," playing on the name of the ailment, appendicitis, discovered for the first time in treating King Edward VII in 1902. "The Pendyces are not only an 'appendix,' redundant in the national organism, but have become infected."[18]

The beautiful, unhappily married woman in *The Country House* is Helen Bellew. She is invited to visit the Pendyce estate because she is a relative of the mother of the family, Margery Pendyce, a fading beauty who is herself less than happy in her marriage to Horace Pendyce, the stubborn, self-centered, and prejudiced squire. Helen captivates George, the elder son of the family. Her husband, the reprobate Captain Bellew, has made her life miserable. She has no means of her own and thus cannot get free of him. Consequently, she incites George to stake his prize-winning racehorse so that they may have a future together. They go to London, but their liaison is discovered and Captain Bellew plans to sue for divorce. Squire Pendyce is horrified that the family name could be sullied in the scandal of a divorce case and threatens to disinherit George. Margery, a gentle person modeled in part on the author's mother, with a reserve of strength that surprises herself, daringly journeys to London to save her favorite son by asking Helen to set him free. The pusillanimous George has not been man enough for Helen anyway, and so she throws him over. Finally, Margery persuades Helen's husband with humility instead of words not to institute the divorce proceedings. He relents, saying, "You're the only Lady I know!"[19]

Galsworthy is somewhat easier on the landed gentry than he is on the urban bourgeoisie, perhaps because he knew them only slightly, through his mother's family connections, or more likely, because he cared for them even as he sometimes deplored their mores and their values. Galsworthy certainly had the ability to be on both sides at once. With him, however, it was a sense of fairness and a depth of vision, not equivocation. By the time he wrote *The Country House* he was a fierce advocate of animal rights, and yet he could both disparage and admire a character thus: "There was no species of beast, bird or fish, that he could not and did not destroy with equal skill and enjoyment" (*CH,* 12); and with fine irony show the pleasure and the horror of shooting:

George felt the ground with his feet, and blew a speck of dust off his barrels, and the smell of the oil sent a delicious tremor darting through him. Everything, even Helen Bellew was forgotten. Then in the silence rose a far-off clamour; a cock pheasant skimming low, his plumage silken in the sun, dived out of the green and golden spinney, curled to the right, and was lost in the undergrowth. Some pigeons passed over at a great height. The tap-tap of sticks beating against trees began; then with a fitful rushing noise a pheasant came straight out. George threw up his gun and pulled. The bird stopped in mid-air, jerked forward, and fell headlong into the grass sods with a thud. In the sunlight the dead bird lay, a smirk of triumph played on George's lips. He was feeling the joy of life. (*CH*, 26–27)

The main weakness of *The Country House* relates to the central dilemma of Galsworthy's life and art: although the novel does make a succinct and valid attack on the complacent roots of English society, showing its isolation from the important social issues of the day, its insensitivity to human needs and frailties, its lack of compassion, its selfishness, and its self-righteousness, nevertheless *The Country House* also shows that the author's sympathies were torn between the old and the new, the haves and the have-nots, the conservative past and the radical present. If only the best of the past could be served while the needs of the present were met.

Fraternity, dedicated to Galsworthy's fellow dramatist J. M. Barrie, and partly based on Turgenev's *On The Eve* (1859), was first begun under the title "Shadows," which the author abandoned on learning that it was being used by another writer. It is set in the Kensington section of London, which housed an upper-middle-class, intellectual, artistic neighborhood adjoining a brooding slum. In the wealthy part abide Hilary and Bianca Dallison, who pale before, and try to avoid, the vibrant life of the poor. Even Hilary's overbred, tiny bulldog, Miranda, shrinks from life:

Miranda found what she had been looking for all her life. It had no smell, made no movement, was pale-grey in colour, like herself. It had no hair that she could find; its tail was like her own; it took no liberties, was silent, had no passions, committed her to nothing. . . . "I would love to live with you. Shall I ever find a dog like you again?" . . . Miranda saw that it had wheels. She lay down close to it, for she knew it was the perfect dog.[20]

Edward Wagenknecht cites this passage to support his statement that "at its best, Galsworthy's symbolism is wonderfully effective."[21] Indeed, symbol, character, and plot all serve well this strong satire of the liberal mind, worried by the misery it sees about it, but more concerned with finding some amelioration that will not disrupt society. *Fraternity* attacks those who eat well and sour their food with a dash of guilt. Celia, Bianca's sister, considers whether to buy another new dress: "But I don't know whether I ought to buy it, with all this distress about!" (*F*, 2). She finally decides on it because: "I am thirty-eight. . . . I cannot afford to lose my husband's admiration. The time is on me when I really must make myself look nice!" (*F,*3). She demands of a seamstress that the dress be ready in just a few days, even though the shop is very busy, and on her way out thinks, "That poor girl looks very tired; it's a shame they give them such long hours!" (*F,* 4).

Hilary and Bianca are a sterile couple, sexually incompatible. He is a writer of independent means. She is a painter and uses a pretty young girl from "the shadows," that is, the slums, as a model. Hilary takes the girl under his wing, and she cleverly wins his heart both by her total acceptance of his control and by her gratitude. He obtains work for the model as a copyist. His wife, however, bristles over his innocent affection and his attempt to help one real human being instead of supporting causes with lofty ideals at safe distances. The young girl, however, is predatory and overplays her hand. She offers herself to Hilary with a kiss too free and too soon. With sensibilities outraged, he reverts to his previous unhappy state of frustration and futility.

Fraternity was attacked as a revolutionary and dangerous book, even though the subject of the satire was not the political control and moral indifference of the ruling classes, but rather the atrophy of intellectuals and their inability to take action against the sea of social problems that surrounded them. Galsworthy was boldly attacking the very people who made up his intellectual and social circle. In a word, he was satirizing himself. In both life and art, he could only visit the slums; he had to accept the sad truth for him that, as Leon Schalit states, "from the world of over-culture no bridge leads to the world of under-culture though the two live side by side."[22]

There is a sexual charge in *Fraternity,* perhaps even more than in *The Man of Property* and *The Country House,* despite their plots of adultery. Even Galsworthy's most vitriolic critic, D. H. Lawrence, whose critical essay on him attacks him in almost scatalogical language, admits to the sexual ingredient in the book, although he calls it "damp and muzzy."[23] Still the combination of a provocative sexual situation, fine characterization, and social criticism keep *Fraternity* fresh and readable.

By the time he was penning *The Patrician,* in 1910, Galsworthy had become a veritable writing machine, working simultaneously on the novel, the play *Justice,* the short stories that would appear in *A Motley* (1910), and several essays. He also maintained a prodigious correspondence. Furthermore, he and Ada were traveling frenetically and hobnobbing with the upper echelons of English society, the patricians (the first title for the new novel). He would maintain this writing pace and style of life for most of the rest of his life. Galsworthy was writing too much, and he was proudly associating with those classes who were the subjects of his satire. The edge of his social criticism began to dull as the Edwardian Age died with the old king in 1910 and a stasis of purpose set in.

Galsworthy was aware that his satiric powers were declining. He wrote in his diary: *"The Patrician* is less satiric than the others. There has been a steady decrescendo in satire through the whole series, and, I think, a steady increase in the desire for beauty."[24] The author slowly but surely substituted an aesthetic quest for beauty for the socially purposeful creation of satire, perhaps partly because of his friendship with the future poet laureate John Masefield, who made the revering and honoring of beauty the central theme in his post-Edwardian poetry and prose.[25]

The writing of *The Patrician* essentially marked the end of the mentorship of Edward Garnett. The editor believed that Galsworthy, in slipping away from social satire of the class he really knew and understood, was veering off in a direction that could only distance him from the source of his creative power: his conflict with the middle-class establishment. Galsworthy, on his part, strongly defended the authenticity of his new novel and the validity of his new direction. They would remain friends, but the relationship was never the same.

The Patrician, like *The Country House,* is the tale of an old landed family, this time the Caradocs of Monkland Court, not willing or able to change with the times. It is a family that lives for leadership and power, and its life-style is depicted by Galsworthy in a fashion more suitable for Victorian than Edwardian times. Miltoun, eldest son of Lord Valleys of the Caradocs, is the hero seemingly destined for a brilliant career in Parliament. But he is a tortured soul, because, like other Galsworthy protagonists, he is desperately in love with a beautiful, unhappily married woman, Audrey Noel, who is separated from her clergyman husband.

Miltoun is one of Galsworthy's impersonal heroes, a product, in part, of the influence of French naturalism, one of what William C.

Frierson calls "central characters of mixed qualities."[26] Miltoun's family, especially his grandmother, Lady Casterley, battle his seeming self-destructiveness. A revealed relationship with a woman in an ambiguous position would seriously damage his chances of winning his seat in Parliament, which is all-important to the family. Like Mrs. Pendyce before, Lady Casterley decides to go herself to talk Mrs. Noel into ending her relationship with Miltoun. It turns out that Audrey has no intention of interfering in her lover's career and is willing either to remain in the background or give him up altogether.

However, Miltoun, like King Edward VIII later, is unable to live without the woman he loves. He cannot pursue his career, for which, in truth, he is not temperamentally suited, without her emotional sustenance. Torn by internal conflict, he becomes seriously ill, and Audrey is summoned to nurse him back to health. This she does but then exits his life by leaving the country. He returns to public life and the ascetic nature that his love affair had nearly mitigated.

The Patrician, the next to the last of the fine series of novels of social criticism, is Galsworthy's most Hardy-like work. It is apparently set in the west country, Galsworthy's ancestral home, and its plot is dark and tragic. The central weaknesses of the novel are the waning of Galsworthy's satirical bent and his mixed feelings toward the landed aristocracy, but its evocation of English landscape and country life is exquisite:

Down by the stream it was dappled, both cool and warm, windless; the trees met over the river, and there were many stones, forming little basins which held up the ripple, so that the casting of a fly required much cunning. This long dingle ran for miles through the foot-growth of folding hills. It was beloved of jays; but of human beings there were none, except a chicken-farmer's widow, who lived in a house thatched almost to the ground, and made her livelihood by directing tourists, with such cunning that they soon came back to her for tea.[27]

Galsworthy continues to add to his gallery of brilliantly achieved elderly characters. In *The Patrician,* Lady Casterley "was that inconvenient thing—an early riser. No woman in the kingdom was a better judge of a dew carpet" (*P,* 95).

The Freelands was started in the spring of 1913, three-fourths finished by the outbreak of war in August 1914, and then rushed to conclusion so that money could be quickly raised for the war effort. It contains the portrait of his dying mother as Frances Freeland, and another critical one of himself as Frances's son Felix, a middle-aged successful writer in a period of stagnation, staleness, uncertainty, and some self doubt: "His eyes, Freeland gray, were a little buffed over by sedentary habit, and the number of things that he was conscious of . . . that the people passing him were distressingly plain, both men and women; plain with the particular plainness of those quite unaware of it."[28]

The novel was a failure when published. It was too late. The British reading public was not interested in its subject, the tyranny of the squirearchy over agricultural workers, when the problem seemed moot, with the workers and the sons of the landed gentry fighting side by side in France. Considered with the preceding novels of social criticism, however, it holds up well.

The Freelands is partly based on Turgenev's novel *Virgin Soul* (1876) and other work by the Russian.[29] It is the story of the efforts on the part of Sheila and Derek Freeland in behalf of tenant farmers, especially Bob Tryst, father of three, who is evicted from his farm for opposing Lady Malloring. The Freelands, a family based on Galsworthy's mother's family, the Bartleets, take the Trysts into their own home. Young Derek, having absorbed his mother Kirsteen's radical views, is inflamed by the injustice he sees around him and, unfortunately, makes a passing suggestion that retaliation should be taken. The excitable Tryst sets fire to the Malloring hayricks and is arrested and imprisoned. The agricultural workers attempt to unite and take collective action against the oppressive land owners, but they are neither well organized nor well led and their efforts fail. Tryst dies trying to escape, and all are left with a sense of futility and despair.

Galsworthy, more so than even in *The Country House* and *The Patrician,* put his profound affecton for English land and the English farmer in *The Freelands.* The opening is reminiscent of both Thomas Hardy and the American poet Edwin Markham's poem "Man with the Hoe" (1899), itself based on Millet's painting showing a brutalized peasant "bowed by the weight of centuries." The novel begins:

One early April afternoon, in a Worcestershire field, the only field in that immediate landscape which was not down in grass, a man moved slowly athwart the furrows, sowing, swinging his hairy brown arm with the grace of strength. He wore no coat or hat; a waistcoat, open with a blue-checked cotton shirt, flapped against belted corduroys that were somewhat the colour of his square, pale-brown face and dusty hair. His eyes were sad . . . his mouth heavy lipped, so that, but for the yearning eyes, the face would have been almost brutal. He looked as if he suffered from silence. The elm-trees bordering the field, though only just in leaf, showed dark against a white sky. . . . The green Malvern hills rose in the west; and not far away, shrouded by trees, a long country house of weathered brick faced to the south. Save for the man sowing, and some rooks crossing from elm to elm, no life was visible in all the green land. (*FR*, 1)

Frances Freeland, mother of four sons, is another fine portrait in Galsworthy's gallery of older people. She is the exemplary Victorian mother living in Edwardian times; seeing her influence diminish; struggling to be useful to the young; generous; sure in her convictons; fastidious; sometimes domineering; often humble; and always sensing that she is the backbone of the family.

The plot of *The Freelands* is melodramatic and obvious. Galsworthy is really not good here at depicting the life of the tenant or transcribing their dialect, even though his affection for them is deep and sincere. Nevertheless, *The Freelands* is the most straightforward and unequivocating, in taking on a distinct social issue, of all Galsworthy's novels of social criticism.

Clearly, in the pre–First World War novels of social criticism, from *The Island Pharisees* through *The Freelands,* Galsworthy attained the peak of his artistry as a novelist. Only immediately after the war, when he was completing the second and third novels in *The Forsyte Saga,* did he approach the craftsmanship, if not the irony and subtlety, of this earlier work.

The Romances

The quest for beauty won out over social issues and class criticism. The reasons: first, Galsworthy, along with many other intellectuals and artists, was sickened and disillusioned by the butchery and waste of the war, so that his faith in the possibility of social progress was irrevocably shaken, and he turned to the emotional problems of individual humans instead of the social problems of conflicting classes; second, the author and his wife now moved in a rarified social circle— opened to them by Galsworthy's literary and financial success and by the fading memory of their affair and Ada's divorce—so that he began to sympathize and later identify with those who had been the prime subjects of his satire. *The Dark Flower* opened the new way.

John Galsworthy published three romances in the period between

1913 and 1919, and these novels, poor as they are in comparison to
the earlier novels of social criticism, nevertheless are his major literary
efforts during that part of his career in which the war was the central
event. They are *The Dark Flower* (1913), *Beyond* (1917), and *Saint's
Progress* (1919).

Galsworthy chose as the subject of the first of his novels of love the
emotional life of a man like himself, an artist who has had few affairs
of the heart but each of great significance in his life. Mark Lennan's
emotional life is presented in three parts: "Spring," "Summer," and
"Autumn." In "Spring," young Lennan, a nineteen-year-old Oxford
student, falls deeply in love with his tutor's wife. She finally gives
him up so that he can marry a girl nearer his age and more appropriate for him. In "Summer," at the age of twenty-six, close to the age
at which Galsworthy met Ada Cooper, Lennan falls passionately in
love with an unhappily married woman in Monte Carlo, who drowns
just after they have consummated their love affair and are about to
elope. In "Autumn," Lennan is forty-six, approximately the age at
which the author met Margaret Morris. The artist becomes obsessed
with the reciprocated love of an uninhibited seventeen-year-old girl,
although he is still married to the wife of his youth. He struggles and
overcomes the temptation in order to return to his wife. The symbolic
dark flower, standing for the natural life-force of passion and carnal-
ity, is first the withered carnation thrown by the tutor's wife from a
departing train, then the dark red carnation found on the body of
Lennan's drowned lover, and finally the dying fire in the hearth near
his wife's bed in which she lay sleeping: "There was no warmth in
that fast-blackening ember, but it still glowed like a dark-red
flower."[30]

The structure and theme of this novel seem to derive from his
friend Arnold Bennett's book *Sacred and Profane Love* (1905), which
depicts the three emotional crises in the life of its heroine. Galsworthy's book is the superior because of its greater sincerity, finer prose,
and more profound insight into human nature.

For *The Dark Flower* "Galsworthy felt a rather special affection."[31]
It was after all a chance to explain his own life to himself. He was
very disappointed, even baffled, over the storm of protest his book
provoked in the Mrs. (and Mr.) Grundys of his time. After all, he
had abandoned social criticism for beauty and love. But they accused
him of advocating free love and condoning adultery. He was, in fact,
merely arguing that marriage without mutual deep love is a hollow

and hypocritical relationship. Furthermore, marital relationships can wear down in time, he argues, and it is only human that a marriage partner could be tempted to seek renewal of inspiration through another love.

Of course the contemporary reader is not the least bit shocked by *The Dark Flower.* That reader, however, finds the book episodic in construction, with only the hero as architectonic. Furthermore, there is a lack of resolution. The novel ends with Mark's wife knowing of his love for the young girl. Can the couple ever again have an emotional relationship with each other?

Perhaps the saving grace of *The Dark Flower,* besides its great sincerity, is the touching beauty of Galsworthy's skillfully executed prose, as when Mark, in "Summer," realizes he has fallen in love:

> He stood on the edge of the little cliff above the road between the dark mountains and the sea black with depth. Too late for any passer-by; as far from what men thought and said and did as the very night itself with its whispering warmth. And he conjured up her face, making certain of it—the eyes, clear and brown, and wide apart; the close, sweet mouth; the dark hair; the whole flying loveliness.
>
> Then he leaped down into the road and ran—one could not walk, feeling this miracle, that no one had ever felt before, the miracle of love. (*DF,* 112)

In *Beyond,* Galsworthy is somewhat indebted to both de Maupassant's *A Woman's Life* (1883) and Bennett's *The Old Wives' Tale* (1908), which also owes a debt to the de Maupassant work. The shared idea was to make a sensitive, intelligent woman and her romantic life the focus of the novel. It was the first time Galsworthy used a woman as protagonist, and he would only do so once more, in *Maid in Waiting* (1931). Galsworthy's story is somewhat more optimistic and less cynical than the French novel and more romantic than Bennett's.

Gyp, the heroine, is a young, vital, beautiful girl burdened by her powers of attraction, which are beyond her control. She is the illegitimate child of a retired army officer, deeply loved by her father. She is frantically wooed by a brilliant but amoral Swedish violinist, Fiorsen, and they marry, but Gyp is unhappy with his overbearing vanity, his cruelty, and his dissoluteness, and after two years she leaves with her infant daughter. She then falls in love with a young upper-middle-class barrister, Bryan Summerhay, and lives with him as his wife. She, however, is temperamental, jealous, and demanding.

Their marital life disintegrates. Bryan dies in a riding fall and Gyp contemplates suicide, but she recovers her emotional health and seeks new purpose in life in helping others. As much as anything, her father's love sees her through her crisis.

The father, Charles Winton, is a literary relation to Soames Forsyte, and his doting love for Gyp foreshadows Soames's relationship with Fleur. Again Galsworthy is quite successful with minor characters, and his loving descriptions of the English countryside are as moving as ever:

She came in at the far end of the fields they called "the wild." A rose-leaf hue already tinged the white cloud-banks, which towered away to the east beyond the river; and peeping over the mountain-top was the moon, fleecy and unsubstantial in the flax-blue sky. It was one of nature's moments of wild colour. The oak-trees above the hedgerows had not lost their leaves, and in the darting rain-washed light from the setting sun, had a sheen of old gold with heart of ivy-green; the half stripped beeches flamed with copper; the russet tufts of the ash-trees glowed. And past Gyp, a single leaf blown off, went soaring, turning over, going up on the rising wind, up—up, higher-higher into the sky, till it was lost—away.[32]

This passage not only serves as fine, mood-setting description, it also symbolizes and foreshadows the death of Summerhay.

As first published, *Beyond* is the author's longest single novel. He revised and cut it drastically, believing that it was his worst-written book.[33] In its revised format it is tight and reads well. Galsworthy had rushed the book for American serialization to obtain money for the British war effort. Given more time and his usual two or three full drafts, the book would have been stronger and tighter at first publication and received more favorably. *Beyond*'s lack of success is due to the fact that younger novelists in England were turning more and more to the inner life of their protagonists, while Galsworthy, in the romances, gave more and more emphasis to plot and description.

Saint's Progress is the last of the three romances, which in 1931 would be collected under the title *Three Novels of Love*. It is the only Galsworthy novel that deals directly and seriously with the First World War. It was, of course, written during the conflagration. This time the author pits passion against orthodox religion, and makes his most direct and most negative comment on the church. In this, Galsworthy owes something to a novel he praised: Samuel Butler's *The Way of All Flesh* (1903). Both books attack religious extremes, moral pretenses, and societal hypocrisy. Both are about clergyman fathers and their attempts to control the thoughts, attitudes, and morality of their children.

Saint's Progress takes place in England in midwar. Noel, daughter of a Church of England clergyman, is in love with an officer about to leave for the front. They wish to marry, but the clergyman, Edward Pierson, refuses permission, so Noel defies him by making love with her soldier in the shadow of Tintern Abbey. She becomes pregnant, he dies in France, and Noel has an illegitimate son.

Pierson is the "saint" who is provided several opportunities to give up his aestheticism, his love for form and ceremony, and to face reality and become a humanitarian. But his is no "pilgrim's progress" toward a new understanding. All his natural decency, goodness, gentleness, and sense of beauty are wasted because of the religious imperatives that deny him an understanding of the modern world and the needs and sensibilities of his fellow human beings. At the end, in self-exile for his failure as moral leader of his parish of hypocrites, he goes out to Egypt as an army chaplain and tries to bring the comfort of his belief to a dying young soldier: " 'O God! Let me be of some help to him!' . . . A flicker of humour, of ironic question, passed over the boy's lips. Terribly moved, Pierson knelt down, and began . . . praying. . . . In the boy's smile had been the whole of stoic doubt, of stoic acquiescence. It had met him with an unconscious challenge; had seemed to know so much."[34]

The "saint" has learned nothing. He does not understand the world and never will.

On the other hand, Noel, although she cannot pray, can say yes to life, find love and happiness again, and, most important of all, survive spiritually and emotionally. She is the symbol of the new generation, the children of the war and afterward; her father is the symbol of the Victorian past, rigid, conforming, and condemning. In *Saint's Progress*, Galsworthy makes his passage to the other side; he will no longer focus on the Victorians or even the Edwardians. His main subject in the novels to come will be the present as seen through sensitive, contemporary eyes.

A remarkable aspect of *Saint's Progress* is that although it was written at the height of the war, and although the novel is pervaded by the fears, shocks, and sorrows of the conflict, it is without hatred of the Germans. The novel emphasizes the humanity of all who are combatants. He deplores the hate vented on innocent Germans and Austrians (like his brother-in-law) by cowardly noncombatant mobs in London. As Leon Schalit says, "The most beautiful thing in the work is the love of humanity."[35]

Before returning to the Forsytes and their adventures in postwar England, Galsworthy wrote one other novel, *The Burning Spear* (1919), a satirical work, which he first published as "recorded by A. R. P——M." Later editions would bear his name. The book is a short, strange, comic satire on the war, seemingly the work of an exhausted, bitter writer needing to relieve his feelings at the end of a long period of psychological enervation. The novel was an abject failure, and it is seldom included in studies of Galsworthy's novels.

Structured on Cervante's *Don Quixote,* and to a lesser extent on Charles Dickens's *Pickwick Papers, The Burning Spear* is the story of John Lavender, a man too old to fight in the war, but driven half crazy by the propaganda he reads every day in five newspapers. Hoping to join in the paroxysm of enmity, lies, insults, and nonsense being spouted, he becomes a voluntary propagandist for the "Hymns of Hate" and embarks on a series of quixotic misadventures. He even has a Sancho Panza–like servant, Joe, and a Dulcinea named Aurora. In the end, disillusioned, he plans an auto-da-fé in which he will immolate himself on a vast pile of newspapers full of the propaganda which has made him mad. In the nick of time Aurora saves her beloved "Don Pickwixote" from the flames.

Like almost all Europeans at the war's end, Galsworthy felt betrayed, humiliated, and angered at the way they had been manipulated by politicians and generals into supporting the absurd, near suicide of Western civilization. Although less than most, Galsworthy too had been swept up in the propaganda mills and used. *The Burning Spear* was an expectoration of self-disgust and a shudder of horror at the way humans allow themselves to be abused. Like Lavender, Galsworthy wanted to cry out, "Countrymen, I know not what I think."[36]

In a period of approximately twenty-one years, from the writing of *Jocelyn* to the composition of *The Burning Spear,* Galsworthy served his apprenticeship as a novelist, rose to eminence as an Edwardian novelist, developed and then abandoned the theme of societal conflict and failure that had made his reputation, and embraced the theme of man's search for beauty, a course which led him to five critical failures in a row, so that the public began to think of him more as an effective and interesting playwright and short-story writer than as a novelist. Then came that fateful day in 1918 when Galsworthy conceived the idea of continuing the story of the Forsytes with a trilogy.

William C. Frierson accounts for the popularity of the novels from *The Island Pharisees* (1904) through *The Patrician* (1911): "He had begun to write social criticisms when the French naturalists had prepared a ready public. He attacked the unimaginative, possessive Englishman of his day, but he was not content with indictment. He suggested an ideal of sympathy, generosity, and liberal values in line with the most enlightened Edwardian opinion. He suggested an awakening but no precise change or alteration."[37]

Furthermore, Galsworthy seemed less radical than others like H. G. Wells. He was after all Harrow and Oxford and a son of the establishment. He was a critic from within who wrote the King's English without improprieties. Of all those English novelists, young and old, writing in that period, including Wells, Bennett, Conrad, E. M. Forster, Woolf, and D. H. Lawrence, Galsworthy was the most accessible.

Chapter Three
The Forsyte Saga

John Galsworthy's crowning achievement is the long story of the Forsyte family, which in the dedication to the second family trilogy, *A Modern Comedy* (1929), he refers to as "The Forsyte Chronicles."[1] These chronicles, like the chronicle histories of the sixteenth century or even the medieval *Anglo-Saxon Chronicles*, span a long period of history. Although not written in chronological order, they begin with the arrival in London of the family founder, "Superior Dosset" Forsyte, in 1821, six years after the end of the Napoleonic Wars, and continue to the death of the chronicles's protagonist, Soames Forsyte, in 1926, eight years after the end of the First World War. The chronicles, although uneven, are one of those cases in literature when the whole is greater than the sum of the parts.

To read the chronicles in historical order, one starts with the stories collected in *On Forsyte 'Change* (1930), beginning with "The Buckles of Superior Dosset, 1821–1863"; slips "The Salvation of Swithin Forsyte," first published in *A Man of Devon* (1901), in between "The Hondekoeter, 1880" and "Cry of Peacock, 1883"; goes on to *The Man of Property* (1906); then to the fragment "Danae," which Ada published in *Forsytes, Pendyces, and Others* (1935), and which was the aborted start of what would become *The Country House*, and where George Forsyte (son of Roger), later to be transformed into George Pendyce, is the young man in love with the married beauty; slips back to more stories in *On Forsyte 'Change;* next reads "Indian Summer of a Forsyte," first published in *Five Tales* (1918); then on to "Soames and the Flag, 1914–1918" in *On Forsyte 'Change;* then *In Chancery* (1920), the interlude *Awakening* (1920), and *To Let* (1921); finally *The White Monkey* (1924), the interlude "A Silent Wooing" in *Two Forsyte Interludes* (1927), *The Silver Spoon* (1926), the interlude "Passers By" in *Two Forsyte Interludes,* and *Swan Song* (1928).

This chapter discusses those works which Galsworthy brought together as that part of "The Forsyte Chronicles" he published as *The Forsyte Saga:* the keystone work, *The Man of Property;* "Indian Summer of a Forsyte"; *In Chancery; Awakening;* and *To Let.* It is an ironic saga, without heroes or epic battles, but still the story of an Anglo-Saxon family representative of a great people. Galsworthy set out to satirize, but twelve years and a terrible war intervened, and he ended by sympathizing. Nevertheless, he produced the finest written portrait of the passing from power of England's upper middle class, people who make money and property the measure of all things, and who value not individual valor but the long steady family march toward riches, in which endurance is the cardinal virtue.

"Forsytism" esteemed the family collective over the individual member; it coveted property, particularly houses; it was determined to survive, as evidenced by the longevity of its practitioners. " . . . when a Forsyte died—but no Forsyte had as yet died; they did not die; death being contrary to their principles, they took precautions against it, the instinctive precautions of highly vitalized persons who resent encroachments on their property."[2]

The Industrial Revolution produced Forsytism. Forsytes were the upwardly mobile, acquisitive, new rich of peasant stock who made their money in the economic growth of London and England. Forsyte families were not old families with ties to the land. Like most modern industrial people, they had no intimate connection with nature, no ability to create beauty, no aristocratic traditions of service, self-sacrifice, and honor. They were not landed gentry; they were people of stocks, bonds, mortgages, and cash, and they believed money could buy anything.

The Man of Property

The Man of Property, which Galsworthy first planned to call "The Forsyte Saga" long before he envisioned a trilogy, was influenced by Tolstoy's *Anna Karenina* (1873–75), a novel he would write an admiring preface to long after his novel of an unhappily married woman and her adulterous affair. Tolstoy's suffering heroine kills herself by throwing herself under the wheels of a train. In Galsworthy's first draft, he had his suffering heroine's lover commit suicide by throwing himself under a horse-drawn cab, but changed to a suspicious accident in the final version. Both novels feature rigid, unsympathetic husbands.

The Man of Property opens in June 1886, at the gathering of the Forsyte clan, at the home of Old Jolyon, to celebrate the engagement

of his granddaughter, June, child of young Jolyon, to the architect
Philip Bosinney, an outsider to the clan. "The Forsytes were resentful
of something, not individually, but as a family. . . . For the first
time, as a family, they appeared to have an instinct of being in contact with some strange and unsafe thing" (*MP*, 5). Old Jolyon's
nephew, Soames, the thirty-one-year-old successful notary, is the perfect Forsyte. He is wealthy, slender, pale, rather bald, strong
chinned, and always impeccably dressed. Moreover, he has, after several vain attempts, married a great beauty, Irene, whom he considers
as much his property as his stocks and bonds and the paintings he
collects and sometimes sells at great profit.

Irene was only twenty-two at marriage, the daughter of a poor,
widowed professor, and she was quite incompatible with her step-
mother. She did not love Soames, but yielded to his persistent blan-
dishments partly out of a need for security. Now Soames is sexually
frustrated by his wife's coldness. He finds he cannot fully "possess"
her. As if to place her like a jewel in a superbly expensive setting, he
commissions Bosinney to build him a mansion at Robin Hill. Irene
and the architect fall in love and begin an affair. She denies herself to
Soames, who yearns for her all the more. Galsworthy exquisitely describes Irene's joy in her love affair and her revulsion for her husband:

She came in with her latch key, put down her sunshade, and stood looking at herself in the glass. Her cheeks were flushed as if the sun had burnt
them; her lips were parted in a smile. She stretched her arms out as though
to embrace herself, with a laugh that for all the world was like a sob.
Soames stepped forward.
"Very-pretty!" he said.
But as though shot she spun round, and would have passed him up the
stairs. He barred the way.
"Why such a hurry?" he said, and his eyes fastened on a curl of hair fallen
loose across her ear.
He hardly recognised her. She seemed on fire, so deep and rich the colour
of her cheeks, her eyes, her lips, and of the unusual blouse she wore.
She put up her hand and smoothed back the curl. She was breathing fast
and deep, as though she had been running, and with every breath perfume
seemed to come from her hair and from her body, like perfume from an
opening flower.
"I don't like that blouse," he said slowly, "it's a soft, shapeless thing."
He lifted his finger towards her breast, but she dashed his hand aside.
"Don't touch me!" she cried.

He caught her wrist; she wrenched it away.
"And where may you have been?" he asked.
"In heaven—out of this house!" (*MP*, 275)

Convinced that Bosinney is his wife's lover, Soames decides to take revenge in a material way by bankrupting the architect for exceeding instructions. Eaten alive by his jealousy and sexual longing for the dark-eyed, blonde woman whom he believes he owns, Soames one night makes his way into her room, now usually locked to him, but accidentally left open, and rapes Irene. He claims his property. Now convinced that she cannot stay with Soames, Irene tells Bosinney what has happened to her. The architect is shocked, stunned, and horrified. Wandering in a London fog, he is run over and killed. Irene returns to Soames "like an animal wounded to death" (*MP*, 373). Young Jolyon, old Jolyon's son, fond of Irene, has come to solace her, but Soames slams the door in his face at the novel ends.

The characterization in *The Man of Property* is superb. The family lives. Soames is one of the great fictional characters of twentieth-century English literature. He is a prototype who, like a Hamlet, a Sherlock Holmes, a Leopold Bloom, takes on an existence of his own beyond the confines of the story or stories in which he appears. Irene, who moves like a vision through the *Saga,* is the only controversial figure in the book. She represents what is perhaps Galsworthy's sole experiment in writing. Quite deliberately he presented her with no clear personality of her own. She is seen and sensed by other characters. Some critics have called this decision an artistic failure. Others have argued that Irene has the infinite variety of true beauty; she is a different dream of loveliness to different men and also to the individual reader.

In order to avoid seeming preachy about subjects he felt strongly about, such as the right of women to their own bodies, the hypocrisy of the upper middle class, and the lack of beauty in the urban world, Galsworthy devised what he called the "negative method." In characters like Soames he presents "the negative, quasi-satiric, which shows what men might be, by choosing defective characters and environments and giving their defects due prominence."[3]

In *Love in the Western World,* Denis de Rougemont says that "passion and marriage are essentially irreconcilable. Their origins and their ends make them mutually exclusive. Their co-existence in our

CARNEGIE LIBRARY
LIVINGSTONE COLLEGE
SALISBURY, N. C. 28144

midst constantly raises insoluble problems, and the strife thereby en-
gendered constitutes a persistent danger for every one of our social
safeguards."⁴ Galsworthy obviously considered this seeming irrecon-
cilibility a major problem for twentieth-century society, and he would
treat this theme again in such works as *The Country House, Fraternity,
The Dark Flower,* and indeed all through the chronicles. Passion, so
desirable for inspiration, purpose, and quality of life, nevertheless
threatens marriage as the bedrock social institution of Western society. In the course of the chronicles, Galsworthy would swing from an
all-out commitment to passion over marriage to the reverse position,
as Soames slowly metamorphoses from villain to hero and the work
evolves from tragedy to comedy.

"Indian Summer of a Forsyte"

The Man of Property was a critical success, and Galsworthy considered a sequel but put it off for some twelve years in order to scrutinize
other sectors of Edwardian society. In 1917 Galsworthy decided to
resurrect the Forsytes in a story. With it he staged a comeback as a
fiction writer. That effort, "Indian Summer of a Forsyte," would
cause the author one year later to plan to expand *The Man of Property*
into a trilogy. "Indian Summer of a Forsyte" links *The Man of Property*
to *In Chancery,* as the story *Awakening* links *In Chancery* to *To Let,* all
five pieces forming the *Saga.*

"Indian Summer of a Forsyte" is a long story of great lyrical quality. The time is the summer of 1892, and old Jolyon Forsyte is
eighty-five. In a belated search for beauty he has purchased Robin
Hill, the mansion that had been so much a part of Irene's and Soame's
grief. Irene, now nearly thirty, has decided to re-enter life. The
reader learns to his surprise that she left Soames the very same night
her lover died and has been living alone, remembering Bosinney, and
earning her keep by giving piano lessons. Unobtrusively, she visits
the grounds of Robin Hill to remember the joy of her only love, is
seen by old Jolyon, and they become friends. Irene, although a Victorian, is called "the lady in Grey" and described as the ideal Edwardian beauty as she walks with the admiring old man who comes to
love her: "She moved beside him. Her figure swayed faintly, like the
best kind of French figures; her dress, too, was a sort of French grey.
He noticed two or three silver threads in her amber-coloured hair,
strange hair with those dark eyes of hers, and that creamy-pale face.

A sudden sidelong look from the velvety brown eyes disturbed him. It seemed to come from deep and far, from another world almost."[5]

The presence of beauty, in the form of Irene as well as in the configuration of the house Bosinney built so lovingly, rejuvenates old Jolyon so that his last few months of life are among his best. He dies sitting under a tree on his lawn with his faithful dog at his feet, waiting for his beautiful friend.

The shift in tone from *The Man of Property* to "Indian Summer of a Forsyte" is staggering. The novel is satiric and ultimately tragic, ending with the horror of poor Irene having no other place in life but to return to the protection, and by implication the abhorred bed, of her insensitive and cruel husband. In the idyllic story, Soames is absent, the satiric edge is blunted, and it appears that Galsworthy has simply abandoned the implied tragic denouement of the novel. Irene has done quite well on her own. We may either conjecture that Galsworthy is no longer angry at his wife's first husband or, more probably, that because of the war it had become possible to believe that a young woman could indeed survive on her own without the protection of a father or husband.

Significant for the developing chronicles, the author brings back to life not only old Jolyon and Irene, but also young Jolyon and his children, Jolly and Holly, foreshadowing the love between him and the ever-enigmatic Irene, as well as the affairs of the next generation.

In Chancery

As the *Saga* continues, Soames remains "in chancery" with the expression's many meanings fitting his situation, including his being in litigation and in a hopeless bind. *In Chancery,* dedicated to Jessie and Joseph Conrad, begins in 1895 and ends with the birth of Soames's only child, Fleur, in 1901, the year the old queen died as the Boer War raged on. For Galsworthy, Victoria's death had marked the end of the age he grew up in and which he used as the background for most of his fiction and all of the *Forsyte Saga* through *In Chancery.* Not surprisingly, he describes with great feeling Victoria's funeral, so shortly to be followed by the death of Soame's father, James, almost the last of the old Forsytes:

There it was—the bier of the Queen, coffin of the Age slow passing! And as it went by there came a murmuring groan from all the long line of those who watched, a sound such as Soames had never heard, so unconscious, primitive, deep and wild, that neither he nor any knew whether they had joined in uttering it. . . . Tribute of an Age to its own death. . . . The hold on life had slipped. That which had seemed eternal was gone! The Queen—God bless her! It moved on with the bier, that travelling groan, as a fire moves on over grass in a thin line; it kept step and marched alongside down the dense crowds mile after mile. It was a human sound, and yet inhuman, pushed out by animal subconsciousness, by intimate knowledge of universal death and change. None of us—none of us can hold on forever.[6]

From the post–World War I perspective, the death of Victoria was the watershed event that separated the world of their fathers from their world and that of their children.

Early in the novel, Soames, who has been on his own since Irene left him some twelve years earlier, and who is frustrated sexually despite visits to prostitutes, frustrated emotionally because of his need for tenderness and long-term female companionship, and frustrated dynastically because he desires a son to carry on the family name and preserve and add to the accumulated property, would like to marry Annette Lamotte, a French girl whose mother keeps a restaurant in Soho. It would be a marriage of convenience if not love. Soames would obtain a virginal young girl who could bear him a son, a source of new vitality for the forty-five-year-old. Annette would obtain a life of luxury. Again Soames, so wise in business, is foolish in human relations; again a woman is to be bought. Of course, he will never obtain the deep, selfless love of a woman he longs for. That cannot be purchased. That is not property.

Regardless, Soames cannot marry until he divorces Irene, whom he has not divorced previously for several reasons: fear of embarrassment from publicity that might adversely affect his law career, a glimmer of hope that they might start over again, and his dislike of the thought of someone else possessing that beauty that once was his. Legally, divorce would be difficult; twelve years have passed since her adultery and new grounds are needed. Hoping that Irene might have a lover, he visits her to propose divorce, only to have his passion for her flame up: "Memory, flown back to the first years of his marriage, played him torturing tricks. She had not deserved to keep her beauty—the beauty he had owned and known so well. And a kind of bitterness at the tenacity of his own admiration welled up in him. . . . The mere sight of her, cold and resisting as ever, had this power to upset him utterly!" (IC, 535–36).

Fearful of Soames, Irene flees to Paris. He suspects that young Jolyon, now fifty, the widowed painter who is Irene's trustee and friend, is also her lover. In the most seriocomic incident of the book, the jealous husband has his wife shadowed by a female private detective. Soames falls into the trap he has laid when he goes to Paris to try a last plea for reconciliation and is taken to be Irene's lover by the detective. Graham Greene would incorporate this humorous plot twist in *End of the Affair* (1951). Soames's importuning drives Irene into young Jolyon's arms, and she takes refuge with him at Robin Hill. But now Soames had grounds, and biting the bullet, he obtains a divorce in the absence of Irene and Jolyon, who have gone to Italy. Now he is "out of chancery." He marries Annette in Paris so that the Forsytes will not know she comes from Soho. Soames's father, old James, is happy at the prospect of a grandson to maintain and increase family property. Annette, however, has a daughter, Fleur, and Soames lies to his father on his deathbed, telling him that a son was born. Irene and Jolyon also have married, and they have a son, Jolyon, called Jon for short.

The subplot of *In Chancery* is very important for the continuation of the chronicles into the next generation. Soames's sister Winifred's ne'er-do-well husband, Montague Dartie, abandons her for a Spanish dancer with whom he runs away to Buenos Aires. She begins a divorce action, under Soames's advice, but Dartie returns to England, "unpressed, unglossy . . . twisted, raked and scraped . . . squeezed . . . like an orange to its dry rind" (*IC*, 663). Winifred takes him back, for like a true Forsyte, she refuses to lose her property to someone else. Meanwhile, their playboy son, Val, an Oxford student, and Holly, young Jolyon's daughter by his second wife, fall in love. Holly's twenty-year-old brother, Jolly, has the old reciprocated Forsyte antipathy of the Jolyon line for the James line, and so, antagonistic to his flamboyant cousin, he dares to him to enlist in the army with him to go fight the Boers. Val agrees. Holly also goes out as a nurse, and in South Africa Holly and Val marry, but poor Jolly dies of typhoid fever.

The love affair of these younger Forsytes is handled well by Galsworthy. He was able to portray the young as well as the old, not only of the Victorian age but also the Edwardian and Georgian periods. Holly's and Val's story also prepares us for the more important love between the next James-Jolyon protagonists, Fleur and Jon.

Soames, now the hero of the *Saga,* has the last word and the last scene of *In Chancery*. He has a child now, albeit a girl: "The sense of triumph and renewed possession swelled within him. By God! This thing was his!" (*IC,* 766).

In Chancery does not have the tragic intensity, the satiric edge, or the sense of drama of *The Man of Property,* but it is equally rich in characterization, it has the gripping power of a fine narrative, its plots are skillfully interwoven, and it shows Galsworthy to have developed an ironic humor that adds subtlety and faceting to the *Saga.* Sympathy for Soames takes root. It becomes apparent that although he shall have no woman's love and no son, he will carry on the indomitable family spirit, ever illustrating that particular English characteristic, that bulldog trait called endurance.

Awakening

In the interlude *Awakening* youth and beauty begin to move from the wings to the center stage of the *Saga.* In a somewhat overly sentimental fashion, Galsworthy describes the life of the eight-year-old Jon Forsyte, son of Irene and young Jolyon, at Robin Hill. It is based on the author's sad recollections of his own childhood at Coombe Warren and the absence of affection from his mother. The story moves the chronicles along to 1909. Jon, who has been born with the proverbial silver spoon in his mouth, is awaiting the return of his fifty-two-year-old father and thirty-eight-year-old mother from a visit to Ireland.

Jon is not a spoiled child and has already learned something of the vicissitudes of life when at seven his governess had "held him down on his back, because he wanted to do something of which she did not approve. The first interference with the free individualism of a Forsyte drove him almost frantic. There was something appalling in the utter helplessness of that position, and the uncertainty as to whether it would ever come to an end. . . . He suffered torture at the top of his voice for fifty seconds. Worse than anything was his perception that 'Da' had taken all that time to realize the agony of fear he was enduring. Thus dreadfully was revealed to him the lack of imagination in the human being!"[7]

The Forsyte love of independence is a consummate English trait, and it represents another way in which, on the symbolic level, the author links the natural attributes of the Forsyte family to his nation's needs, values, and character. Another lifetime longing of the Victorian-born Englishman was the need for affection from his busy, household-running mother, so soon to send him off packing to boarding school. But Jon has the goddess Irene for a mother, with "hair like Guinevere's, and clutching it, he buried his face in it" (*A,* 60). Learning from his mother that Daddy is not in her room tonight, the Oedipal child is allowed in Beauty's bed:

"Oh! Mum, do hurry up!"

"Darling, I have to plait my hair."

"Oh! not to-night. You'll only have to unplait it again to-morrow. I'm sleepy now; if you don't come, I shan't be sleepy soon."

His mother stood up white and flowey before the winged mirror: he could see three of her, with her neck turned and her hair bright under the light, and her dark eyes smiling. It was unnecessary, and he said:

"Do come, Mum; I'm waiting."

"Very well, my love, I'll come."

Little Jon closed his eyes. Everything was turning out most satisfactory, only she must hurry up! He felt the bed shake, she was getting in. And, still with his eyes closed, he said sleepily: "It's nice, isn't it?"

He heard her voice say something, felt her lips touching his nose, and, snuggling up beside her who lay awake and loved him with her thoughts, he fell into the dreamless sleep, which rounded off his past. (*A,* 62–63)

The writing here is so unselfconscious that all Freudian snickers are repressed. The story is sentimental, but it is also delicate, dreamlike, and enrapturing. Like Eugene O'Neill's play *Ah, Wilderness* (1934), it is more a tale of how a writer would have liked his childhood to be than how it was. It is also the story of when and how a child comes to know the importance of beauty in life.

To Let

With *To Let,* Galsworthy leaps a chasm. *In Chancery* ends with the birth of Fleur in 1901; *Awakening* takes place in 1909. *To Let,* written in 1921, jumps the *Saga* to 1920. Galsworthy thus avoids almost the whole Edwardian period and the First World War. Clearly, the author was fed up with the war and all the books about the conflict too. Interestingly, he gauged his audience perfectly. The British reading public, still grieving the loss of nearly a million young men, felt the same way. They wanted to read about the postwar world, and Galsworthy catered to their and his own needs. Thus structurally, *To Let,* the postwar novel, fits better with *A Modern Comedy,* the postwar trilogy, than it does with *The Forsyte Saga.*

To Let continues that perennial conflict in the chronicles: the war between Forsytism and beauty. Soames does battle again with Irene and Jolyon, and the battleground is the romance between their children, Fleur and Jon, a battlefield the older generation tries unsuccessfully to obscure with the smoke of ignorance and parental disapproval. And the weight of old grievances and injustice will crush young love.

The story opens with a chance encounter. Soames and his eighteen-year-old daughter, Fleur, the only child he shall ever have, meet Irene and her nineteen-year-old-son, Jon, in a place of beauty, an art gallery. Soames is a collector. Young Jolyon, of course, is a painter. The children fall in love, like Romeo and Juliet, at first sight. Also coming onto the scene is Michael Mont, the young aristocrat who will marry Fleur on the rebound.

Fleur, attractive, willful, restless, and spoiled, has completely captivated her doting father. She is the treasured possession of his life now. He and Irene, as well, both of whom have assiduously avoided any contact with each other for years, are disturbed by the obviously fateful meeting and attraction of the second cousins. Unwisely, the children have never been told a word of the family feud, and the hints and dark illusions only prick their curiosity and drive them together.

Along with her love for his father, the kindly, gentle, poetic Jon is the great joy of Irene's life. She, seen through Soames's eyes, is still a great beauty: "Her profile was so youthful that it made her grey hair seem powdery, as if fancy-dressed; and her lips were smiling as Soames, first possessor of them, had never seen them smile. Grudgingly he admitted her still beautiful and in figure almost as young as ever."[8]

Jolyon wants to tell Jon about the past, but Irene disallows it out of fear that Jon might misjudge her motivation for betraying Soames. Jon and Fleur meet again, and their feelings for each other deepen. The clever Fleur makes inquiries and begins to learn the reason for the parental enmity. Determined to have possession of Jon—she is after all the child of Soames Forsyte—Fleur proposes a secret marriage to Jon. Although he loves the girl passionately, he cannot bring himself to hurt his parents in this way. As is, his father, now well past seventy, is grieved by the fateful turn of events and finally has a heart attack in the same place his own father did, the garden of Robin Hill:

He paused a minute with his hand on the rope of the swing—Jolly, Holly—Jon! The old swing! And suddenly, he felt horribly—deadly ill. "I've over-done it!" he thought, "by Jove! I've over-done it—after all!" He staggered up towards the terrace, dragged himself up the steps, and fell against the wall of the house. He leaned there gasping, his face buried in the honeysuckle that he and she had taken such trouble with that it might sweeten the air which drifted in. Its fragrance mingled with awful pain. "My Love!" he thought: "The boy!" And with a great effort he tottered in through the long window, and sank into old Jolyon's chair. The book was there, a pencil in it; he caught it up, scribbled a word on the open page. . . . His hand dropped. . . . So it was like this—was it? . . . There was a great wrench; and darkness. (*TL,* 1033–34)

The word was surely *Irene.* Like his father, young Jolyon dies with the thought of beauty, with the vision of Irene in his mind. Irene's gentle, passive, unblemished, Greek-sculpture loveliness remains a constant male dream, a male ideal of unchanging pulchritude. It is unreal, of course, but it is irresistible. Irene, passing through the chronicles, is almost as much an architectonic as Soames is.

However, just before dying, Jolyon has written Jon explaining everything and asking Jon not to hurt his mother with this marriage. The boy decides to break off with Fleur. Ironically, Irene and Jolyon, who had battled family and convention in their own love affairs and marriages, now use family and convention to keep their child from the girl he loves, while the hidebound, conventional Soames, out of love of his unhappy daughter, reluctantly goes to Irene to ask her to allow the marriage, promising never to bother her again. Irene leaves it up to Jon, who again rejects the idea.

Fleur must have a man to possess, and so she now accepts the suit of Michael Mont, whom she does not love. Jon and Irene move to Canada, while Robin Hill, a rich man's setting for a beautiful wife, an artist's gift of love to his beloved, old Jolyon's last but happiest home, the joyful domicile of young Jolyon, Jolly, Holly, Irene, and Jon, is finally to let.

Soames has lost his sting. There is great sympathy for him as he buries his Uncle Timothy, the last of the old Forsytes, and as he strives to make Fleur happy. The To Let sign up over Robin Hill is also, symbolically, up in Soames's heart. That is, he has at long last abandoned ownership as a goal per se. He especially no longer believes he can possess people, neither Irene, nor Annette, nor Fleur. As in the last words of the novel and the *Saga,* "He might wish and wish and never get it—the beauty and the loving in the world" (*TL,* 1104). His seeming change of character is partly due to the emergence of what is best in the Forsytes: honesty, fair play, courage, and endurance.

To understand Soames, and later Fleur as she matures in *A Modern Comedy* and takes center stage in the chronicles, one needs to consider the words of Galsworthy's friend, the French critic André Chevrillon, as he explains that the complexity of the English character may be fathomed "if you understand how by one of those odd mixtures of contraries produced by life, that species is a combination of the aristocratic and the vulgar, the commercial and the puritanical, the gregarious and the individualistic, the haughty and the mean, the primitive and the over-civilised."[9] *In Chancery* and *To Let* blunt and dissipate the tragedy and the satire of *The Man of Property*, but because of Galsworthy's ever-sharpening storytelling skills and brilliant use of the omniscient-author technique, the reading audience is drawn into what has become a family epic, stripped of tragic connotation, yes, but fascinating nevertheless because it is more than the recounting of a tragic marriage, more than a single extended family's tale; it became the saga of the English people as they passed through the valley of death into the modern world. The public eagerly waited for more.

The Forsyte Saga brought John Galsworthy international renown. From the year of its publication, 1922, the author was considered the leading British novelist and a major spokesman for his craft and his country. The great appeal of the *Saga* remains to this day. It is a fascinating story, rich in texture, character, and detail, to which readers return again and again to refresh the images of that captivating family, the Forsytes. It is one of those long tales that have a lifelong holding power. Forsyte 'Change is always in business between the covers of a waiting book.

Chapter Four
The Forsytes Revisited:
A Modern Comedy

A Modern Comedy is a "comedy" in the manner of Honoré de Balzac's *The Human Comedy,* a long prose work work with lengthy novels connected by shorter pieces, recreating society at a particular period and depicting characters of different positions, occupations, and classes. Galsworthy's concatenate format repeats that of the *Saga:* satiric novel, lyric interlude, satiric novel, lyric interlude, and concluding satiric novel. The trilogy is set in an extremely narrow time span: *The White Monkey* in 1922–23, *The Silver Spoon* in 1924–25, and *Swan Song* in 1926. Galsworthy is indeed now writing chronicles: the novels are published two years after their time; his materials are the current event and the immediate observation.

In *The White Monkey,* Fleur is the leading woman, but the spotlight shifts to her aristocratic young rival, Marjorie Ferrar, in *The Silver Spoon.* She takes center stage again in *Swan Song.* Soames now shares the limelight with Michael Mont, Fleur's understanding, sympathetic, but unloved husband, as the key male figure in the trilogy. Jon and Irene are featured in the interludes, "A Silent Wooing" and "Passers By," and Jon again plays a chief part, along with Fleur and Soames, in *Swan Song.*

Despite Galsworthy's readers' interest in the fate of Soames, Fleur, Irene, and Jon, *A Modern Comedy* is less successful than *The Forsyte Saga.* It lacks the keystone of a great work like *The Man of Property.* The author, reacting to a political shift to the left in Britain, changes from a critic of the upper middle class and the aristocracy to their supporter. Surely money and power did not need his help. Soames, still the man of property, as Old Jolyon had christened him in the first novel of the *Saga,* is now become something of a victim as property is under attack in modern Britain.

Moreover, Galsworthy is unsure of his purposes. Initially his intention is to substitute for the previous attacks on Forsytism, a satiric evaluation of modern literature and art, the devil-may-care attitude of

the flappers in post–World War I London society, and politicians
who either catered unconscionably to the masses or dreamed up impossible utopian schemes out of feelings of guilt or out of naive social-
istic conceptions. He cannot bring it off, and early in *A Modern
Comedy* Galsworthy shifts tone and focus to the less topical, more archetypal conflict between generations and to the development of plot
and character. However, a sense of pervading despair is the residue of
the misattempt at general satire, and the reader begins to question,
along with the author, the meaning of life in so frenetic and value
denying a world.

The White Monkey

"When *The White Monkey* was published, the surprising discovery
that the ageing Galsworthy (by then fifty-seven) could understand the
wildness and intellectual freedom of the generation of young people
liberated from war caused most comment."[1] Wryly, he has Fleur decide "not to have more than three styles in her house: Chinese, Spanish, and her own."[2] She knows how to vamp men: "Conscious of
Wilfrid biting his lips, of Sir Lawrence taking that in, of the amount
of silk leg she was showing, of her black-and-cream teacups, she ad-
justed these matters. A flutter of her white lids—Desert ceased to bite
his lips; a movement of her silk legs—Sir Lawrence ceased to look at
him" (*WM*, 9). The early part of the novel justifies Galsworthy's dedicating it to the satirist Max Beerbohm, but the cleverness fades and
the plot is slow in unfolding.

However, it is in chapter 6, when Soames appears, that the Forsyte
fan warms to the story as he watches the one-time villain, now with
his Victorian standards and values thoroughly approved by the author, inching his way into the modern world. It is he, Soames "the
undertaker" who has arranged so many Forsyte funerals, who sees the
painting in the bedroom of his dying cousin, George, that is the chief
symbol of the book: "Over the fireplace was a single picture, at which
Soames glanced mechanically. What! Chinese! A large whitish sidelong monkey, holding the rind of a squeezed fruit in its outstretched
paw. Its whiskered face looked back at him with brown, almost human eyes" (*WM*, 65).

The monkey represents modern man, the ageing, post-Darwinian
primate, left with only the refuse of his heritage and looking bewildered. Soames buys the painting at a a sale and gives it to Fleur for

her Chinese room. It is his unconscious reproof of her time and her life-style. Without prewar spiritual values, without belief in the greatness of human capabilities, with only sybaritic goals, the post-war generation is superficial, lost, bewildered, unfulfilled. It is a generation, for Galsworthy, without the necessary hope and the illusions of civilization, such as chivalry, comity between the sexes, honest dealings between humans, and sexual fidelity.

As the story opens Fleur has lived with her husband, Michael Mont, for two years. To the disappointment of her father, Soames, and her father-in-law, Sir Lawrence Mont, she has not become pregnant. Like Soames she is a collector, but not of pictures. She collects celebrities, among whom is the disillusioned young poet Wilfrid Desert, a friend of Michael, but determined to make Fleur his lover. Still disappointed over her unrequited love affair with Jon Forsyte, now living with Irene in British Columbia, she is not capable of loving her doting husband, who soon learns he was a runner-up choice. Fleur is torn; she wants the adventure and delicious excitement of a love affair, but she is too conventionally middle class to really give in, so she keeps the frustrated Wilfrid at arm's length even while visiting his apartment. Meanwhile, Michael is aware of what is going on but he decently, if painfully, insists: "It's all right, Fleur. You must do what you like, you know. That's only fair" (*WM*, 126). Michael does seem to be a man fifty years ahead of his time.

Fortunately for the miserable Michael, Wilfrid gives up the chase and decides to go abroad. Fleur is pregnant with Michael's child and the couple turn to each other. A son, "the eleventh baronet," is born. "Fleur raised her head, and revealed the baby sucking vigorously at her little finger. 'Isn't he a monkey?' said her faint voice" (*WM*, 246).

Soames meanwhile has his own plot. He is a member of the board of directors of an insurance company, where he discovers that the company manager is dishonest. Soames exposes him, but the manager escapes and the shareholders wish to blame the directors for the ensuing losses. Ever the proud and upright Forsyte businessman, Soames, who in fact has practically saved the company, resigns with a flourish, much to the loss of the shareholders.

There is yet a third plot, melodramatic like Soames's, and sexual like Fleur's. Tony Bicket, a packer in Michael's publishing firm, has stolen to buy extra food and medicine for his beautiful, young wife, Victorine. Fired, he takes to peddling balloons on the street. Not knowing why her husband was fired, Victorine goes to Michael for help. Appreciating her beauty, he sends her to an artist friend to model for dust jackets. The artist, a decent chap, convinces the reluctant woman to pose nude for a painting. The extra money will help the young, working-class couple leave "this awful little room, this awful country" (*WM*, 196). They hope to emigrate to Australia. But Victorine is ashamed to tell her husband that she has posed in the nude. His working-class sensibilities preclude understanding the artist's professional distance from, and respect for, his model. Bicket sees the painting in a gallery and is infuriated. Michael helps him to understand, however, and when he realizes that his wife did not sleep with the painter and that she had posed to get him off the streets, he relents and they reconcile.

The story of the mutual sacrifice of honor for a loved one is touchingly sentimental and reminiscent, save for a Christmas setting, of O. Henry's "The Gift of the Magi." The Bickets, however, are less than fully believable. Galsworthy's sympathy for their class, without a real knowledge of its problems and its poverty—as well as its prejudices—appears somewhat patronizing.

The White Monkey, after a false start, is a strong, well-plotted work of irony. Galsworthy sympathizes with Soames's Victorian bewilderment at the inevitable new values and new tempo of life, but at the same time indicates his awareness of what is good in the new freedom. Michael is less rigid, more sensitive, and every bit as decent a representative of his generation as Soames is of the older one. It is Fleur, half English, but also half French, spoiled and vacuous, who is made to symbolize the chaotic in post–World War I English life.

"A Silent Wooing"

It is February 1924, and Jon Forsyte has moved from British Columbia to South Carolina to grow peaches. The twenty-three-year-old has recovered from his ordeal with Fleur, and now he meets nineteen-year-old Anne Wilmot, a South Carolinian of good family, and they fall in love while getting lost horseback riding under the stars. In this interlude Galsworthy not only links *The White Monkey* with *The Silver Spoon* but he also takes the opportunity justly to criticize the American penchant for violence, particularly the many lynchings of blacks in the South at that time. Unfortunately, Galsworthy's knowledge of Southern aristocracy is as superficial as his acquaintance with the English poor. He has all his white Americans constantly saying "I reckon" and, shades of Stephen Foster, they are still talking about their "darkies." Nevertheless, the story is idyllic and poetic, short of dialogue, long on feeling. Thus the title, "A Silent Wooing."

The Silver Spoon

It is now September 1924, and Michael has left publishing and has permitted himself to be nominated to a Conservative Party seat in Parliament, where he hopes to support a new but hairbrained plan for social reform called Foggartism, after its creator, Sir James Foggart, and perhaps modeled satirically after Fabian Socialism, espoused by George Bernard Shaw and other friends and acquaintances of Galsworthy. Furthermore, by making Michael a politician, Galsworthy is able to expound some of his own pet social theories on the social and economic problems of Great Britain—problems he continually worried about—including overpopulation and the need to make the nation agriculturally more self-sufficient.

Fleur enjoys collecting celebrities and running an artistic salon, until she runs afoul of the loose-living, easy-spending, popular aristocrat Marjorie Ferrar, who spitefully and anonymously publishes a thinly veiled attack on Fleur's salon and her husband's support of Foggartism. Attending Fleur's next at home, Marjorie makes a snide remark that is overheard by Soames, who, much to Michael's consternation and Fleur's regret, shows the young woman to the door, calling her a traitress. Fleur also counterattacks with letters to friends commenting on Marjorie's immorality, and she finds herself on the receiving end of a libel suit. In order to keep his daughter out of court, Soames offers a compromise settlement, but it is refused and the suit goes to trial.

The law suit is the heart of *The Silver Spoon,* a title, of course, symbolizing being born to luxury and indolence, as both Fleur and Marjorie were. Galsworthy, the former barrister and son of a solicitor, was well able to make a courtroom scene exciting both in fiction and on the stage. Furthermore, at the heart of the law suit is the interesting conflict between the upwardly mobile, still rising upper middle class and the aristocracy. Soames's daughter, having married into the upper class, is pushing too hard for social recognition and is scoffed at by the establishment. Marjorie, granddaughter of an earl, is immoral; that is, she belongs to the class that has always believed it could do anything it pleased with anyone it chose. Fleur is still middle-class. She is bound by conventions and would only have an affair as a secret and dangerous romantic adventure.

The clever Soames has Marjorie's past and present investigated, and enough evidence turns up to prove immorality. In court, Fleur's counsel cross-examines Marjorie so well that she is left without any reputation to speak of. The case is a public sensation. Proud Marjorie refuses to deny that she has ever had a liaison, and so with sexual freedom proved, Fleur wins the case, but it is a Pyrrhic victory, for society turns on her and snubs her, whereas Marjorie is more popular than ever.

The central irony of the novel is that the reaction to the trial shows that moral values have revolved 180 degrees from Victorian to Georgian times. Marjorie's revelation of sexual freedom would once have led her to near total ostracism by society, as happened to Ada and John before Ada's divorce. Now Marjorie is a heroine to her sophisticated crowd and Fleur is seen as a prude. Thus Galsworthy, with his Victorian perspective, satirizes the new morality of the younger generation and condemns the very kind of relationship he and Ada engaged in thirty years before as daring young people.

To escape her embarrassment, Fleur wishes to make a trip around the world, ignoring the career of her husband and the needs of her son. Good old Soames will take his daughter on the trip, and Michael, who cannot leave Parliament during term, will join them six months later in Canada. The eleventh baronet is left behind, too. The silver spoon of indulgence has distorted the values of Fleur, a wife and mother who easily leaves her husband and her child to the care of surrogates. As to the generation after:

> "A——a!" said the eleventh baronet, plopping the spoon. The contents spurted wastefully.
> "Oh! You spoiled boy!"
> " 'England, my England!' " thought Michael, "as the poet said."[3]

Galsworthy thus indicated his conviction that the generation born in the 1920s would be more spoiled than Edwardian children. World War II proved him wrong.

The Silver Spoon is a finer satire than *The White Monkey,* primarily because here Galsworthy is on sure ground when he uses the courts, when he works on the further mellowing of Soames, now seventy, and when he discusses changing sexual morals. The strong dramatic central plot, supported by a credible subplot involving Jon Forsyte's brother-in-law Francis Wilmot's unsuccessful pursuit of Marjorie Ferrar, builds suspense, so that the reader is held by unfolding events as well as by convincing insights into upper-class society.

"Passers By"

"Passers By" is Galsworthy's most humorous interlude. Unlike in most of Galsworthy's longer fiction, the viewpoint does not shift from person to person. "Passers By" is told almost entirely from Soames's standpoint. Soames and Fleur are in Washington D.C. on their round-the-world trip. Coincidentally, Jon, Jon's wife, Anne, and his mother, Irene, are also visiting Washington, and Soames discovers this by recognizing his young kinsman in Rock Creek Cemetery before a statue by Augustus Saint Gaudens "of seated woman within the hooding folds of her ample cloak [which] seemed to carry him down to the body of his own soul."[4] Soames assiduously avoids Jon and his wife and then finds out, to his dismay, that they are staying in the same hotel as he and Fleur are. Trying everything to avoid having the depressed Fleur meet her former lover, now obviously happily married, Soames is forced into all kinds of comic subterfuges to keep them apart, and he succeeds. At the end of the interlude, however, when all is safe, he hears a piano played beautifully in a salon. Looking in, Soames realizes it is "*she*! Though he supposed her grey by now, the sight of that hair without a thread in it of the old gold affected him strangely. Curved, soft, shining, it covered her like a silver casque. She was in evening dress, and he could see that her shoulders, neck, and arms were still round and beautiful" (*PB*, 517–18).

Soames is transfixed by this vision from his distant past. Irene is still in his heart, still a cause of grief, still inexplicable to him. "Her face came round in the light. . . . Soames saw it, still beautiful, perhaps more beautiful, a little worn, so that the eyes looked even darker than of old, larger, softer, under the still-dark eyebrows. And once more he had that feeling: 'There sits a woman I have never known.' . . . She had had many faults, but the worst of her faults had always been, was still her infernal mystery!" (*PB*, 518).

It is only when he is safely in bed and near to sleep that Soames realizes that the image of beauty in his heart and mind, refreshed by his unexpected sight of the unsuspecting Irene, is immortal: "*She!* She would never die!" (*PB*, 519). His last thoughts before sleep fuse his vision of Irene and "the great bronze-hooded woman, with the closed eyes, deep sunk in everlasting—profound . . ." (PB, 519). Then sleep. But that statue is not only one of immortal beauty, it is also a vision of death, everlasting and profound. After all it is funereal statuary. Soames is an old man and Galsworthy brilliantly makes Soame's vision of eternal beauty and that of eternal rest conterminous.

Swan Song

Galsworthy continues as a chronicler in *Swan Song* by using as his focusing event the great General Strike of 1926, a national crisis in which nearly all of Great Britain participated either on the side of the strikers or in support of the government by volunteering labor to carry on the essential services of the country. The strike was a test of national character, as Galsworthy well knew, and the British proved themselves able to endure and survive with a minimum of violence what could have developed into a revolution, although the chasm between the working class and the other classes deepened so much that effects of the strike remain to this day.

The strike brings all of the surviving Forsytes together. This time it is Winifred's house, not Timothy's, which becomes Forsyte 'Change. Now Galsworthy has his actors on stage for the resolution of all the residual questions from *The White Monkey:* what is the ultimate fate of Soames, Fleur, Jon, and Irene? Galsworthy even moves the action in part back to the beautiful, but ill-fated country house, Robin Hill, thus connecting the beginning of the *Saga, The Man of Property,* to the end of *A Modern Comedy* and the chronicles: *Swan Song.* As *To Let* leads to the death of Young Jolyon, so *Swan Song* points to the passing of Soames, each of the two men with their respective virtues and shortcomings ever representing the two halves of the Forsyte, or English, character.

Swan Song opens in the spring of 1926 with the General Strike taking place. It ends with the year. In order to help in the crisis, Michael convinces Fleur to start a canteen for volunteer railway workers. Of course his sympathies, and Galsworthy's, are with the government, not the strikers. Meanwhile Jon Forsyte, having sold his estate in South Carolina, and planning to try farming in England, has taken Irene and Anne to visit Paris. Returning to the country for which he has been homesick for nearly six years, Jon volunteers to do his bit in the strike. He visits his stepsister, Holly, and her husband, Val, at Wansdon, where he associates the beauty of the landscape with his old love, Fleur: "Jon lingered five minutes at his window. That orchard in full bloom . . . was as lovely as on that long-ago night when he chased Fleur therein."[5] As Jon falls asleep that night, "a form—was it Anne's, was it Fleur's—wandered in the corridors of his dreams" (*SS*, 539). His love for Fleur has awakened even as he dreams.

Shortly afterward Fleur sees Jon in her canteen, and "it was within her heart as if, in winter, she had met with honeysuckle" (*SS*, 548). He is as sexually appealing to her as ever, even though he is smudged with coal dust and sweat. She does not speak to him and he does not see her. Returning home, "quickly she undressed. Was that wife of his her equal undressed? To which would he award the golden apple if she stood side by side with Anne? And the red spots deepened in her cheeks" (*SS*, 550–51). So sexually aroused, when her husband comes in she gives herself to him with Jon's countenance in her mind.

The astute Soames, ever caring for the daughter he has loved in his middle and later years as much as he loved Irene in his youth, is aware of some odd change in Fleur, who has decided to play with fire and have an affair with Jon. She schemes and plans, invites Jon and Anne to lunch, and sees that they pass Robin Hill where once their stars were crossed. As Fleur closes in on her kill, Soames, realizing what is happening, worries and suffers more and more as he remembers Irene and Bosinney. Now, however, lovers are not brave spirits battling a hostile society, but dangerous violators of the moral code that necessarily protects society.

Meanwhile, Michael has abandoned the social fiasco called Foggartism and devotes himself to aiding the poor directly. He persuades Fleur to help, and she cleverly conceives a plan to found a rest home for working-class girls, financed by her father, located near to Jon at Wansdon. She even learns to drive a car to facilitate her commuting.

Fleur is a true descendent of James Forsyte. When she desires to collect and to have, nothing can stop her, and she is determined to have Jon as her lover, despite, and because of, his attempts to reject her obvious advances. Finally, her opportunity arrives. She has offered Jon a ride, and she stops near fateful Robin Hill again. With consummate irony Galsworthy has Fleur seduce, nearly rape, Jon with the same possessive intensity that her father raped Jon's mother:

> Jon reached his hand up. She turned her lips and touched it.
> "Jon—kiss me just once."
> "You know I couldn't kiss you 'just once,' Fleur."

"Then kiss me for ever, Jon."

"No, no! No, no!"

"Things happen as they must—you said so."

"Fleur—don't! I can't stand it."

She laughed—very low, softly.

"I don't want you to. I've waited seven years for this. No! Don't cover your face! Look at me! I take it all on myself. The woman tempted you. But, Jon, you were always mine. There! That's better. I can see your eyes. Poor Jon! Now, kiss me!" In that long kiss her very spirit seemed to leave her; she could not even see whether his eyes were open, or, like hers, closed. And again the owl hooted.

Jon tore his lips away. He stood there in her arms, trembling like a startled horse.

With her lips against his ear, she whispered:

"There's nothing, Jon; there's nothing." She could hear him holding-in his breath, and her warm lips whispered on: "Take me in your arms, Jon; take me!" The light had failed completely now; stars were out between the dark feathering of the trees, and low down, from where the coppice sloped up towards the east, a creeping brightness seemed trembling towards them through the wood from the moon rising. A faint rustle broke the silence, ceased, broke it again. Closer, closer—Fleur pressed against him.

"Not here, Fleur; not here. I can't—I won't—"

"Yes, Jon; here—now! I claim you."

* * * * * * * *

The moon was shining through the tree stems when they sat again side by side on the log seat.

Jon's hands were pressed to his forehead, and she could not see his eyes.

"No one shall ever know, Jon."

He dropped his hands, and faced her.

"I must tell her."

"Jon!"

"I must!"

"You can't unless I let you, and I don't let you."

"What have we done? Oh, Fleur, what have we done?"

"It was written. When shall I see you again, Jon?"

He started up.

"Never, unless she knows. Never, Fleur—never! I can't go on in secret!"

As quickly, too, Fleur was on her feet. They stood with their hands on each other's arms, in a sort of struggle. Then Jon wrenched himself free, and, like one demented, rushed back into the coppice. (*SS*, 741–42)

Galsworthy discreetly plants a row of asterisks to curtain off part of this unusual scene, but there is no doubt as to who did the violating.

Alas for Fleur, as it happened to Soames with Irene, in the very act of winning she loses forever what she wanted most, for Jon will never be her lover again:

> She stood trembling, not daring to call. Bewildered, she stood, waiting for him to come back to her, and he did not come.
>
> Suddenly, she moaned, and sank on her knees; and again she moaned. He must hear, and come back! He could not have left her at such a moment— he could not!
>
> "Jon!" No sound. She rose from her knees, and stood peering into the brightened dusk. The owl hooted; and, startled, she saw the moon caught among the tree tops, like a presence watching her. A shivering sob choked in her throat, became a whimper, like a hurt child's. . . . What did it mean? Was she beaten in the very hour of victory? He could not—no, he could not mean to leave her thus? . . . Life seemed suddenly to have gone out. (*SS*, 742–43)

Disillusioned, Jon returns home and prepares to confess to Anne, who surprises him with the news that she is expecting a child and that she has instinctively realized what has happened between him and Fleur. Jon begs forgiveness and swears never to see Fleur again, an oath he will keep. Returning to Soames, Fleur's distraught state is obvious to her father. He fears she might harm herself, yet he is relieved that the affair with Jon must be over.

In bed that night something wakes him, and he soon discovers that his picture gallery is on fire. Fleur, in her unhappy state, had dropped a lighted cigarette there. Soames rushes down to his daughter to get her and his grandson out, calls the servants, and runs back to the gallery to save his precious pictures. Choking and nearly blind from the smoke, he saves one picture after another by throwing them out a window. The fire brigade arrives, and Soames is prevented from rescuing his last painting, a copy of Goya's *Vendimia*, emblematic of Fleur. It is left perched on the window ledge when he is dragged down to the air below. The heavy picture is dislodged by a fireman's stream as Fleur, standing below it, looks up. Soames realizes that she wants to be killed: " 'It's falling!' he cried. 'Look out! Look out!' and just as if he had seen her about to throw herself under a car, he darted forward, pushed her with his outstretched hands, and fell. The thing had struck him to the earth" (*SS*, 780).

Galsworthy reminds the reader of the chronicles, as indeed Soames must have been instantly reminded, of the death of Bosinney in *The*

Man of Property. Neither author nor character was going to let someone die for love again except as a sacrifice, one life for another, his
old life for his beloved daughter's young one. And thus Soames, when
he dies of his injury, dies a hero. Ironically, a man of property became
for one brief moment a man of action, "a proper champion," as Sir
Lawrence Mont calls him (*SS*, 794). Not only has Soames saved his
daughter's life, but he has also saved her soul. She is cured of folly
and despair by her father's sacrifice, and the reader may assume that
she will be a good wife and mother from then on, for as Soames lay
dying she begs his forgiveness, tells him that she loves him so, and
"like a little girl she said: 'Yes, Dad; I will be good!' " (*SS*, 792).

   Swan Song is qualitatively second only to *The Man of Property* in the
chronicles, in part because it is a photo negative of the first novel,
published twenty-two years previously: the villain has become the
hero, love for a lost wife is replaced by love for a saved daughter, and
adultery is deplored instead of romanticized. As with *The Man of
Property*, characterization is very sharp, the plot singular and always
interesting, and the description of the English countryside once more
bespeaking the author's great love for the land of his ancestors.

   Forty years have transpired. Soames has expiated his guilt, his
crime against love, although he never realized how he wronged Irene.
The triangles of the *Saga:* Soames—Irene—Bosinney, Soames—
Irene—Jolyon, and the triangles of *A Modern Comedy:* Michael—
Fleur—Wilfrid, Michael—Fleur—Jon have all come undone. The parade of years and characters is all over. The swan song is the Forsytes'
as well as Soames's. Galsworthy has Soames buried under a crab-apple
tree, a favorite Galsworthy symbol for nature and eternally flowering
life. There will be no cross over him, merely a flat stone, for neither
the character nor the author were religious men. Sir Lawrence states
a proper epitaph: "I respected Old Forsyte. . . . He dated, and he
couldn't express himself; but there was no humbug about him—an
honest man" (*SS*, 793).

   Michael sums up Galsworthy's view of life only five years before his
death: "It's pretty hard sometimes to remember that it's all comedy;
but one gets there, you know" (*SS*, 796).

   And Galsworthy added in the preface to *A Modern Comedy:* "There
is still truth in the old proverb: 'That which a man most loves shall
in the end destroy him' "[6] For Soames it was the possession of beauty
and love, not only for the woman of his heart, but also for his child.
Still, finally, a long life ending, even if it has not been an entirely

fulfilled one, is not a tragedy; it is only, like any comedy, an intriguing story. In comedy or tragedy, the hero's character is often the shaper of his destiny. Soames's contradictions—his nearly religious belief in the sanctity of property and his gentlemanly behavior in all situations except his first marriage; his philistinic lust for collecting and his true appreciation for fine art; his competitive Forsyte instinct and his sense of honor and duty—provide the major themes, the central architectonic, and the essence of character development in "The Forsyte Chronicles," and are a major reason Soames Forsyte has a niche in the pantheon of the great, living characters of English fiction. On the publication of *Swan Song* in 1928, London newspapers announced the death of Soames Forsyte with other front page news.

The completion of *Swan Song* and the rapid publication of the trilogy affected all of Europe. There were instant translations into French, German, and other languages. It was widely recognized that the great English family epic, the forty-year historical panorama of a changing nation had been completed. Galsworthy saw the chronicles as his bid for literary immortality. They won him the Nobel Prize.

"The Forsyte Chronicles" truly comes to an end, however, with the publication of *On Forsyte 'Change* (1930), in which Galsworthy backs and fills with pleasant, nostalgic stories, all written after *Swan Song*. They range from stories about the family founder, "Superior Dossett" and Aunt Hester's only love affair, an abortive one with a German army officer in 1845, to the last story and the last word on Soames, "Soames and the Flag," which tells of Soames's and Galsworthy's reaction to World War I, a horrified disgust for the mass slaughter in the trenches and the mistreatment of aliens on the home front, but an understanding of English doggedness that will not permit itself to lose. Soames reflects: "Hold on—until! For never, even at the worst moments, had he believed that England could be beaten."[7] Nineteen pieces in all, dedicated to H. V. Marrott, who would write Galsworthy's official biography after the author's death, they flesh out the lives of such Forsyte stalwarts as James, Old Jolyon, Timothy, Soames, and June, generally by dealing with early, insightful, formative, or humorous incidents in their lives. Galsworthy wrote these stories at the insistence of a vast reading public demanding more Forsyte. They also gave him pleasure and relief as he was struggling with his final work, the story of the less familiar Charwells.

Chapter Five
From Forsytes to Charwells:
End of the Chapter

R. H. Mottram suggests that Galsworthy left the upper-middle-class Forsytes to write about the upper-class Charwells (with their own ancient pronunciation: *Cherrell*) because he was "constrained to correct the very full use he had made of his parternal heritage by turning to his other side, and setting his final trilogy in an atmosphere of those very much older and originally landed . . . maternal relatives. . . . The business of *End of the Chapter* is with the front that the very oldest stratum in English society makes."[1] Although some Forsytes either are mentioned or play a small part in this trilogy without interludes, they are only part of the background to the story. Fleur alone of the clan has a featured role to play because her mother-in-law, Emily Mont, is a Charwell, the sister of the family's head, General Sir Conway Charwell.

The Great Depression began as Galsworthy was working on the first part of the new trilogy. He was very concerned for the growing unemployment, the misuse of the environment, and the possibility of another war, with destruction raining from the sky upon his beloved England. In his discussion in *End of the Chapter* of city-leveling air raids as a part of future warfare, Galsworthy shows a startling prescience. It was partly because of his fears for his native land that he chose to write about a family that he called in a letter to his friend André Chevrillon "representative of the older type of family with more tradition and sense of service than the Forsytes."[2] Thus, to a large extent, *End of Chapter* is a defense of, or an apologia for, the privileged class in post–World War I society, a class the author was not quite born into, but the one with which he associated almost exclusively in the last years of his life, and one which he believed could save the country from spiritual, moral, and political disintegration.

Maid in Waiting (1931)

It is 1928, and the Charwells of Conderford Grange are one of those ancient aristocratic English families who, although they have lost much of their former political and economic power, continue their honorable tradition of service to the nation. General Charwell is retired, but his son, Captain Hubert Charwell, D.S.O., is still a serving officer, although at the beginning of the first novel in the trilogy, *Maid in Waiting,* he is in trouble. On an archaeological expedition in Bolivia, in self defense, he shot and killed a native mule skinner who had mistreated the animals, had been flogged, and then had tried to murder him. Hubert, back home in England, is first unfairly charged by the American professor Hallorsen, the excursion leader, with having caused the expedition to fail by mishandling the transport. Things go from bad to worse for poor Hubert, for no sooner is he cleared of that problem when the Bolivian government charges him with murder and demands extradition. He finds the English government, with its sense of noblesse oblige in world affairs, discounting his explanation of events and bending over backward to seem to be fair to a small nation. The luckless soldier is incarcerated awaiting extradition to Bolivia, and the entire main plot of the novel is the story of the Charwell struggle to save Hubert and the family reputation.

At the heart of these efforts is one of Galsworthy's finest characters and the central figure of the trilogy, Hubert's sister, Dinny Charwell, a maid-in-waiting in the medieval sense of one who serves. Dinny, whose name is really Elizabeth, is Galsworthy's portrait of the ideal English upper-class girl. She is soft, beautiful, charming, intelligent, plucky, brave, enterprising, and never disillusioned. "Dinny was slight and rather tall; she had hair the colour of chestnuts, an imperfect nose, a Botticellian mouth, eyes cornflower blue and widely set, and a look rather of a flower on a long stalk that might easily be broken off, but never was."[3]

Dinny Charwell is, for the first time in the Galsworthy canon, a young heroine without a hidden passion, without neurosis, without guilt. She loves her family, the English countryside, and her ancestral home. She is not in conflict with a father or a husband. She is reasonable and unselfish. And she has a sense of humor. She rejects the marriage suit of Alan Tasburgh, a brave young naval officer, because at twenty-four she is too young to marry, and she also rejects Professor

Hallorsen, who is strong, tall, handsome, decent, but an American, and Dinny could never live far from her native land. No wonder she was adored by the English reading public, who immediately recognized her as one of their own.

Dinny is the chief author of Hubert's rescue, aided by yet another upper-class heroine, Hubert's bride, Jean Tasburgh. Clearly a main purpose of Galsworthy here is to show that women are every bit as capable of striking out for justice and using the system to right wrongs as men are. Furthermore, they accomplish their deeds with quiet bravery and without force. Yet they remain entirely feminine. Hubert, oddly, is almost totally passive in the story, doing practically nothing to save himself. Very few male authors of Galsworthy's generation, or any other for that matter, either saw women or wrote of them in that strong light. Even in a humorous vein, women are shown competent to do what men have traditionally done. Pressed into service on a chase, Fleur not only drives her car with two nonmechanical men as passengers, but she also takes charge of fixing the flat (*MW*, 223).

The main plot of *Maid in Waiting* is almost juvenile. The reader knows from the beginning that Hubert will get off. The back-up plan to rescue him if necessary reads like a story from the *Rover Boys*. The plot is a skeleton for Galsworthy to drape with his belief that Britain was neglecting its "best" class, the dedicated-to-service class, the aristocracy. A democratic reader at the end of the twentieth century finds such a bald defense of privilege anachronistic to say the least. Many of Galsworthy's contemporaries did too. Having battled against privilege in such early work as *The Island Pharisees,* Galsworthy now cynically proposes that service to the state justifies special treatment for those who traditionally have performed it regardless of what crime they may have committed. The old-boy network is expected to look after its own.

Galsworthy has Dinny's Uncle Adrian, a highly respected character, speak for the belief that the upper class, unappreciated though they may be, are best prepared to lead: "You see, there are such a tremendous lot of directive jobs to be done; and the people most fit for such jobs are those who, as children, have had most practice in taking their own line, been taught not to gas about themselves, and to do things because it's their duty. It's they, for instance, who run the Services, and they'll go on running them, I expect. But privilege is only justified nowadays by running till you drop" (*MW*, 143).

When Hubert visits General Charwell's club, that institution is fa-

vorably described in a way that no English writer after Galsworthy
would have dreamed of doing:

> He entered an edifice wherein more people had held more firmly to the prides
> and prejudices of a lifetime than possibly anywhere else on earth. There was
> little however, either of pride or prejudice, about the denizens of the room
> into which he was now shown. A short, alert man with a pale face and tooth-
> brush moustache was biting the end of a pen, and trying to compose a letter
> to 'The Times' on the condition of Iraq; a modest-looking little Brigadier
> General with a bald forehead and a grey moustache was discussing with a
> tall, modest-looking Lieutenant Colonel the flora of the island of Cyprus.
> (*MW*, 129)

The younger generation of male English writers who served in the
First World War, or in the one which followed, would have torn the
club apart and treated the officers sitting about with nothing else to
do but write letters to the *Times* and chat about the flora in Cyprus
as a bunch of Colonel Blimps at best, or very dangerous men of insuf-
ficient intelligence and too much power, as, for example, C. S. Forester portrays General Curzon in *The General* (1936).

The subplot of *Maid in Waiting* is more credible than the main
plot. Dinny's Uncle Adrian has long loved Diana Ferse, whose husband has been confined in a private mental institution for madness.
Her life with him was a living hell, but, although she no longer loves
her confined spouse, she has remained faithful to her marriage vows.
He escapes and, somewhat in control of himself, turns up at his house
insistent on his rights as husband. Galsworthy continues to abhor the
possibility of forced sexual relations between husband and wife.
Dinny knows what may happen. " 'Uncle,' said Dinny, 'the night?'
Adrian groaned. 'That we must save her from this somehow.' " (*MW*,
119) Diane is saved, but poor Captain Ferse loses his life in the course
of their ministrations. As a result, Adrian and Diana must part at
least for a while.

Besides the fine portrait of Dinny, the best aspect of *Maid in Waiting* is the humor. Again Galsworthy draws a superb older person.
This time it is Aunt Em, Fleur's mother-in-law, and she has some of
the funniest lines in the Galsworthy canon, as when she asks, "Where
is Bolivia?"

> "In South America, Aunt Em."
> "I never could learn geography. . . . Once they asked me where
> Livin'stone kissed Stanley, and I answered: 'Niagara Falls' and it wasn't."
> (*MW*, 276)

Galsworthy also enjoys a humorous swipe at modern art. An old marquess is trying to pass off a painting on Sir Lawrence:

"Will you tell me what you think of this?" The Marquess went to the corner, took up a canvas that was leaning against the wall, and brought it to the light. It represented with a moderate degree of certainty a young woman without clothes.
"By Steinvitch," said the Marquis; "she could corrupt no morals, could she—if hung?"
Sir Lawrence screwed in his monocle: "The oblong school. This comes of living with women of a certain shape, Marquess. No, she couldn't corrupt morals, but she might spoil digestions—flesh sea-green, hair tomato, style blobby. Did you buy her?"
"Hardly," said the Marquess: "she is worth a good deal of money, I am told. You—you wouldn't take her away, I suppose?"
"For you, Sir, I would do most things, but not that; no," repeated Sir Lawrence, moving backwards, "not that." (MW, 135)

Still *Maid in Waiting* represents a falling off from *Swan Song*. The novel is too polemical and less inventive than its predecessor. The author is less comfortable with a rare happy ending. Moreover, unlike with the chronicles, the reader feels little liking or sympathy for the characters, with the exception of Dinny, Adrian, and perhaps his brother Hilary, one of the very few sympathetic clergymen in Galsworthy's fiction.

Flowering Wilderness (1932)

The sole plot of *Flowering Wilderness* is even less plausible than the main plot of *Maid in Waiting*. It is 1930, Fleur has had a daughter, Adrian and Diana Ferse have married, and Dinny, now twenty-six, meets the poet Wilfrid Desert, Fleur's former would-be lover, now returned from years of wandering in the desert. They fall in love at first sight and in ten days are engaged. However, Wilfrid is a man with a terrible secret. In the Middle East, at the muzzle of a gun, he abandoned his religion and became a Moslem. As a point of fact, he had no belief before the conversion and has none afterward. He simply did not think that religion was worth dying for when he had no faith in God. He was not a coward; during the war he had been decorated for bravery. As the establishment learns of his action it wonders: "Could young Desert really have betrayed the traditions? It seemed improbable. And yet, in spite of his excellent war record, might there be a streak of yellow in him? Or was it, rather, that at times a flow of revolting bitterness carried him on to complete cynicism, so that he flouted almost for the joy of flouting?"[4]

Wilfrid has written a very fine, personally revealing poem, "The Leopard," which painfully depicts the incident. He shows it to Michael, who feels it must be suppressed to protect Wilfrid and Dinny, but who also realizes its great worth:

> "Magnificent!"
>
> "Yes, but you'd never have done it."
>
> "I haven't an idea what I should have done."
>
> "Oh, yes, you have. You'd never have let sophistication and God knows what stifle your first instinct, as I did. My first instinct was to say: 'Shoot and be damned,' and I wish to God I'd kept to it, then I shouldn't be here. The queer thing is, if he'd threatened torture I'd have stood out. Yet I'd much rather be killed than tortured."
>
> "Torture's caddish."
>
> "Fanatics aren't cads. I'd have sent him to hell, but he really hated shooting me; he begged me—stood there with the pistol and begged me not to make him. His brother's a friend of mine. Fanaticism's a rum thing! He stood there ready to loose off, begging me. Damned human. I can see his eyes. He was under a vow. I never saw a man so relieved."
>
> "There's nothing of that in the poem," said Michael.
>
> "Being sorry for your executioner is hardly an excuse. I'm not proud of it, especially when it saved my life. Besides, I don't know if that was the reason. Religion, if you haven't got it, is a fake! To walk out into everlasting dark for the sake of a fake! If I must die I want a reality to die for." (*FW*, 400–1)

Surely only an English writer, perhaps only Galsworthy, in the early thirties, as Hitler was rising to power and Mussolini controlled Italy, could write, "Torture's caddish" and "Fanaticism's a rum thing!" and suggest that a character might give in to a person threatening murder because he felt sorry for his would-be executioner whose brother was his friend. Moreover, Galsworthy seems creakingly anachronistic to have Wilfrid ostracized by society for having risked lowering English prestige in the Middle East. The cynicism, racism, and hypocrisy which the author is attacking is expressed by Sir Lawrence Mont: "The individual Englishman in the East is looked up to as a man who isn't to be rattled, who keeps his word, and sticks by his own breed. . . . If a single Englishman is found wanting, down goes the stock of all . . . other . . . Englishmen" (*FW*, 415). However those attitudes were pre-Boer War, not post–World War I. Galsworthy was beating a dead horse.

Nevertheless, slowly but surely Dinny's well-meaning family and a cruel and unforgiving society drive the lovers apart. General Charwell screams to Dinny: "He'll be a Pariah!" (*FW*, 422). The reader is reminded of Conrad's young hero who suffers for years for one mistake: Lord Jim. And Galsworthy honestly acknowledges his debt to his deceased friend's novel by mentioning *Lord Jim* (1900) directly in his text (*FW*, 434).

In the end, the suffering Wilfrid leaves Dinny and England for a life of obscurity in Siam. Dinny must slowly recover a desire to live. Once more Galsworthy returns to the sad or tragic ending typical of his long fiction.

As in *Maid in Waiting,* the hero is strangely passive and the heroine is active and aggressive, not only in defending him but also in making sexual advances. Dinny wants very much to make love with Wilfrid, and although he has proposed marriage to her, there is little evidence that he desires to sleep with her:

With her cheek to his she said quietly:
"Do you want me to be everything to you before you marry me? If so, I can."
"Dinny!"
"Very forward, isn't it?"
"No! But we'll wait. You make me feel too reverent."
She sighed. "Perhaps it's best."
Presently she said: "Will you leave it to me to tell my people everything or not?"
"I will leave anything to you." (*FW*, 410–11)

Sex and action seem to have become women's property in the last novels of Galsworthy. It is as if Englishmen are too war weary, too decimated, and too overwhelmed by the sexual revolution to initiate, to change, to create, or, ironically, to do battle any more. When Wilfrid's servant suggests to Dinny that she and his master simply go off together, Dinny replies:

"Nothing I'd like better; only I'm afraid he wouldn't think it proper."
"In these days a young lady can do anything, miss."
"But men still have to be careful, Blore." (*FW*, 481)

When the well-meaning Charwells have almost succeeded in driving Wilfrid off, Dinny makes one last attempt to give up her virginity to her lover and consummate their relationship: "Would you like me to stay here tonight?" she asks Wilfrid. (*FW*, 539) But her exhausted, emasculated lover can only equivocate: "Yes! No! I don't know" (*FW*, 539).

So it is a woman who personifies England in *End of the Chapter*. Dinny is the lover and protector of the family estate. She stands for action. She strives for marriage, children, and regeneration. The great beauty of the countryside is seen through her eyes:

The many miracles of England thronged her memory, while she stood among the old trunks inhaling the lichen-bark-dusted air. Upland grass with larks singing; the stilly drip in coverts when sun came after rain; gorse on wind-blown commons; horses turning and turning at the end of the long mole-coloured furrows; river waters now bright, now green-tinged beneath the willows; thatch and its wood smoke; swathed hay meadows, tawnied cornfields; the bluish distances beyond; and the ever-changing sky—all these were jewels in her mind, but the chief was this white magic of the spring. She became conscious that the long grass was drenched and her shoes and stockings wet through; there was light enough to see in that grass the stars of jonquil, grape hyacinth and the pale cast-out tulips; there would be polyanthus, too, bluebells and cowslips—a few. She slipped on upward, cleared the trees, and stood a moment to look back at the whiteness of the whole. "It might have dropped from the moon," she thought: "My best stockings, too!" (*FW*, 419)

Dinny is a part of that beauty, and her sexuality is much needed if there were to be new generations to love the miracles of England.

Flowering Wilderness shows signs of hasty writing. Some of the dialogue seems almost antediluvian. Galsworthy appears avuncularly fond of his young female characters, particularly Dinny, and quite convinced of the impotence of the young men of his time. Wilfrid's and society's dilemma concerning his conversion at gunpoint seems puzzling to a post–Viet Nam War reader. Yet the author's sensitive, detailed depiction of Dinny's painful, abortive love for her poet, and the dignified but doomed struggle she endures in trying to save him, redeem the novel. Although no Soames Forsyte in richness and complexity, Dinny Charwell, especially in *Flowering Wilderness,* is a major character in twentieth-century English fiction, because, like Soames, she perfectly embodies the hopes, the attitudes, and the accomplishments of a class of people. Soames, however, is deeper, rounder, and protean. Dinny is "the best foot forward."

Over the River (1933)

John Galsworthy's last novel, *Over the River,* was dedicated to Rudolph and Viola Sauter and published posthumously. He barely finished it before rapidly advancing debility stopped his pen. Like Wilfrid the poet, he was about to go over the river and into history. The year is 1931, and the historical event that is the background to this novel is the Great Depression. Once again, as in *The Man of Property,* the main plot centers around an unhappily married woman in dire need of dissolving her brief marriage. This time, as in *The Man of Property,* the lovers are in the right, but unlike in the earlier novel they have not committed adultery. Now the woman in the misalliance is Dinny's younger sister, Clare, who has married brilliantly but unwisely. Her husband, Sir Gerald Corven, a member of the Colonial Service and an empire builder, is seventeen years older than she. He is a sensualist and a sadist who has whipped Clare with her own riding crop and done other things to her which she can neither mention nor abide.

> "There was a lot at first, my riding whip was only the last straw."
> "You don't mean—!" cried Dinny, horrified.
> "Oh! Yes."[5]

After leaving Gerald in Ceylon, Clare meets an impoverished young man, much nearer her own age, on board the ship bringing her home to England. Tony Croom falls in love with her at first sight, but Clare, although enjoying his attentions, nevertheless keeps him at arm's length, having had enough of what she calls "physiology" to last a long time.

Gerald follows Clare back to England, and like a young Soames, tries to take back his property by force:

> A surge of shamed anger stained her cheeks. He had fascinated her; he has used her as every kind of plaything. He had—!
> His voice, cuttingly controlled, said:
> "Well, my dear, you were very sudden." Neat and trim, as ever, and like a cat, with that thin-lipped smile and those daring despoiling eyes!
> "What do you want?"

"Only yourself."

"You can't have me."

"Absurd!"

He made the quickest kind of movement and seized her in his arms. Clare bent her head back and put her finger on the bell.

"Move back, or I ring!" and she put her other hand between his face and hers. "Stand over there and I'll talk to you, otherwise you must go." (*OR,* 641)

Clare has more success in fending off her hated husband than Irene did. She sums up her aversion:

"There are some things that can't be done to me and you have done them."

"I've said they shan't be done again."

"And I've said that I can't trust you." (*OR,* 643)

One time, however, in an exhausted moment of weakness, she does give in to him.

Determined either to have her back or be rid of her, Gerald has Clare and Tony shadowed by a private detective. The young couple are indiscreet in their choice of meeting places, although nothing passes between them but three kisses on the cheek. Clare is not in love with Tony and not interested in an affair, although she plans never to return to her husband. The vindictive Gerald sues Clare for divorce, charging adultery and naming poor Tony as corespondent. The novel builds to the courtroom scenes, which are among the best of many in the Galsworthy canon; particularly exciting are the biting cross-examinations. Gerald wins his false case as his attorney forces Clare to lie about having sex with Gerald the one time after their separation. She tells the lie to save love-struck Tony's feelings, but her sacrifice is to no avail, as the young man senses she is not telling the truth.

After the trial and the divorce, Clare offers herself to Tony, who initially refuses that kind of payment. Clare is always in sexual control of the relationship with Tony, continually putting him off until she wishes to seduce him. Finally she does so, and they become lovers, although she is flippantly condescending about it. She says: "The Ford and I went over. Dinny, we've justified the law. Tony no longer looks like a bereaved orphan. . . . Yes, I prefer him as a lover to a friend" (*OR* 887). They will become part of the modern smart set, having a sexual relationship outside of marriage even though they are single and free to marry. Galsworthy's ending of the main plot is cynical; the courts and society reward dishonesty and promote hypocrisy; and a modern woman may take a lover without loving him.

The subplot focuses on Dinny's slow recovery from her love affair with Wilfrid and her active support of her sister in the law suit. In the midst of the family trouble, she receives the shocking news from Siam that the "Honourable Wilfrid Desert drowned on expedition up country some weeks ago. Body recovered and buried on spot" (OR, 763). Dinny falls desperately ill. Finally her health and will to live return. Moreover, she has a suitor, Eustace Dornford, a barrister and a member of Parliament, who is Clare's employer. He is forty, very quiet and conventional, and he

. . . had an excellent digestion; could eat and drink at all times without knowing anything about it afterwards. He was an indefatigably hard worker even at play. . . . And now, though his practice was going up by leaps and bounds since, two years ago . . . he had stood for Parliament. And yet he was the last sort of man to incur the epithet 'go-getter.' His pale-brown, hazel-eyed, well-featured face had a considerate, even a sensitive look, and a pleasant smile. He had kept a little fine dark moustache. . . . After Oxford he had eaten dinners and gone into the Chambers of a well-known Commons Law Junior. Being a subaltern in the Shropshire Yeomanry when the war broke out, he had passed into the Cavalry, and not long after into the trenches, where he had known better luck than most people. His rise at the Bar after the war had been rapid. Solicitors liked him. He never fell foul of judges, and as a cross-examiner stood out, because he almost seemed to regret the points he scored. He was a Roman Catholic from breeding rather than observance. Finally, he was fastidious in matters of sex, and his presence at a dinner table on circuit had, if not a silencing, at least a moderating effect on tongues. (OR, 664)

Alas for poor Dinny, he is really quite dull after Wilfrid, and she simply slides into marriage with this eligible, if unexciting, man as an anodyne for her loss. She never loves Eustace and probably never shall, but she admires and respects him. The reader wonders if that will be enough?

Again in *Over the River*, women do most of the taking charge, particularly of General Charwell, Dornford, and the helpless and inept Tony. The only strong, decisive man in the novel is the villainous Corven. Also Galsworthy once more pleads nostalgically for the values of England's past. In an epistolary epilogue, Uncle Adrian, while writing fondly about the family estate, is really offering the author's farewell and final accolade to his country and its tradition-bearing aristocracy:

Generations of love and trouble, and goodness knows not too much money, have been spent on it, and the result is something very hand-made and special. Everything's changing, and has got to change, no doubt, and how to save the old that's worth saving, whether in landscape, houses, manners, institutions, or human types, is one of our greatest problems, and the one that we bother least about. We save our works of art, our old furniture. . . . Why not . . . our social life? "The old order changeth"—yes, but we ought to be able to preserve beauty and dignity, and the sense of service, and manners—things that have come very slowly, and can be made to vanish very fast if we aren't set on preserving them somehow. Human nature being what it is, nothing seems to me more futile than to level to the ground and start again. The old order had many excrescences, . . . but now that the house-breakers are in, one does see that you can smash in an hour what has taken centuries to produce; and that unless you can see your way pretty clearly to replace what admittedly wasn't perfect with something more perfect, you're throwing human life back instead of advancing it. The thing is to pick on what's worth preserving. (*OR,* 894)

What clearly was worth saving for Galsworthy was the upper class; not the upper middle, business class of the Forsytes, but the landed gentry with whom the author had hobnobbed for more than ten years, and in whom he saw the only hope of the nation, for they were the class born to lead and to serve selflessly in the government, the church, and the military.

"The Forsyte Chronicles" ends as it began—with a married woman and her lover, an insensitive husband, and the study of class. Law suits and courtroom scenes abound in the chronicles. Galsworthy is satisfied with a successful formula, and he repeats it, unlike the protean Thomas Mann, with whom he is often compared, who could write *Buddenbrooks* (1900) in one decade, *The Magic Mountain* (1927) in another, and *Joseph and His Brothers* (1933–44) through two additional decades.

End of the Chapter and, indeed, the chronicles are best appreciated when taken as a whole. As in Balzac's *the Human Comedy,* the greatness is in the scope and the sweep and the panorama. Galsworthy created and directed a parade: characters, events, and scenes in a pageant of England passing. His facile style in the novel, his direct narrative strategy, his humane outlook, his respect for human dignity, his compassion for person and animal, his ability to create memorable characters, his story-telling skills, and his broad vision of English society will insure him a place among the major British novelists of the twentieth century.

Chapter Six
The Short-Story Writer

John Galsworthy considered the long short story to be "one of the best of all forms of fiction; it is the magic vehicle for atmospheric drama. In this form the writer . . . comes nearest to the poet, the painter, the musician. The tale rises, swells and closes, like some movement of a symphony."[1] The shorter story was a quick-flashing effort "over almost before form is thought of."[2] Galsworthy wrote long short stories, short stories, and sketches, fairly brief descriptions of individuals representing a type or class of people, or personifying an idea, an ideal, or a value. The sketches are carryovers from Victorian literature, with a long ancestry back to the Renaissance writers and even to the ancient Romans and Greeks, but little seen by the time Galsworthy was writing his.

The main preoccupations of Galsworthy's short fiction are love, beauty, the glory of nature, social justice, hatred, old age, the poor, and care for animals. Few of his stories present high adventure. More are either mood pieces or stories of passions in conflict. As his storytelling art developed, he moved away from the French naturalism in vogue at the end of the nineteenth century and wrote stories incorporating careful use of symbols and classical myths.

Galsworthy published fourteen volumes of stories and sketches, two of which, *Two Forsyte Interludes* (1927) and *On Forsyte 'Change* (1930), are part of the chronicles. The fifteenth volume of stories, selected by Ada Galsworthy and titled *Forsytes, Pendyces, and Others,* was published posthumously in 1935. Some of Galsworthy's stories, like "The Apple Tree," are among his most famous works, regularly anthologized and often a part of the curriculum in English-speaking schools the world over.

Galsworthy began as a short-story writer. *From the Four Winds* (1897) brought him some forty reviews, mostly favorable, and convinced him that he could indeed be a writer. Yet, in his 1932 Nobel Prize address, near the end of his life, he would call this collection of nine stories, imitative of Rudyard Kipling and Bret Harte, "that dreadful little book."[3] Galsworthy never revised that first collection

or allowed it to be republished. In fact, twenty-five years after it was
published he bought up the few remaining unsold copies to keep
them out of circulation. Still, it was with the short story that he
chose to begin his apprenticeship in writing. Galsworthy's major
story and sketch collections are *A Man of Devon* (1901), *A Commentary*
(1908), *A Motley* (1910), *The Little Man* (1915), *Five Tales* (1918),
Tatterdemalion (1920), and *Captures* (1923). *Abracadabra* (1924) is a
reprint of the last five stories in *The Little Man. Caravan: The Assem-
bled Tales* (1925) is an anthology containing all of Galsworthy's notable long short stories, with the date of writing affixed to each piece,
thus providing the best single volume opportunity to understand the
development, scope, and achievement of the author as a writer of
short fiction. *Satires* (1927) does much the same thing for Galsworthy's short short fiction and sketches, essentially reprinting *A Commentary* and the "Studies of Extravagance" section of *The Little Man.*

A Man of Devon (1901)

Galsworthy's fourth book, the last written under a pseudonym, is,
like his first, a collection of stories. *A Man of Devon* contains four long
pieces: "A Man of Devon," "The Salvation of Swithin Forsyte," "The
Silence," and "A Knight." The title piece, set in the author's ances-
trial home shire, is an adventure tale of wild love and hate in a lovely
countryside. A beautiful farmer's daughter is distracted from her
young swain by a gun-running, buccaneering sailor. Finally, she is so
upset that she jumps to her death from a cliff. Galsworthy uses the
time-honored, if very old-fashioned, epistolary form, which harkens
back to Samuel Richardson. The letters are written by a visitor who
happens to witness the events. The story is extremely hard to read
because of Galsworthy's strained and unsuccessful attempt to write dialect. Moreover, the work is so imitative of Thomas Hardy that it
accidentally approaches parody.

By far the best and only memorable story in *A Man of Devon* is
"The Salvation of Swithin Forsyte," the first story in what would
eventually be "The Forsyte Chronicles." The story is the initial indi-
cation of great talent in Galsworthy. In it, Old Swithin Forsyte, a
rich man, company director, and a bachelor, is dying alone. He
dreams of an adventure he had as a young man, fifty years before, in
which while traveling in Europe he met and fell in love with a young
working-class girl. Tempted to marry her, he finally realized that it
would not do. She would never be acceptable to his family and class,
and so, by giving her up he "saved" himself at the last moment. The

story, rich in irony, portrays one of Galsworthy's fine old men who "die without seeing sacrifices, chivalry, love, fidelity, beauty, and strange adventure."[4] In other words, Swithin dies without having lived. Rich living is no substitute for an engaged life. The unloved leave life like bubbles breaking in the air. Galsworthy is almost cruel in his depiction of the epicurean bachelor's death. Swithin dies drinking champagne: " 'It isn't Heidseck!' he though angrily. . . . 'But as he bent to drink again something snapped, and, with a sigh, Swithin Forsyte died over the bubbles" (*MD,* 185). And in the end the reader feels both pity and scorn for the old man.

"The Silence" is the Joseph Conrad–like story of a mining engineer's suicide overseas, worn down by a job that forces him to send men to their deaths in deep, unsafe shafts; by the terrible silence of the jungle around him; and by the implacable incomprehension of his masters at company headquarters in London. Once more, an observer, also an engineer, sees, learns, and reveals how far men may be driven even against their nature by those who have power. In the end, after learning of suffering and death, the owners merely remark: "Business is Business! Isn't it?" (*MD,* 219).

Set in Monte Carlo, "A Knight" is the romantic story of an old soldier of fortune who, like the hero of Arthur Conan Doyle's *The Exploits of Brigadier Gerard* (1896), enjoys recounting his past battles and adventures to the narrator. Many years ago, at forty-five, he fell in love with an eighteen-year-old girl, married her, and lost her to a young man. She died leaving a child that is not his but whom the old soldier struggles to support. He is a man, nevertheless, who deeply respects women, and when a woman's reputation is traduced in his presence, he provokes a duel, which he then uses to end his life of heartbroken misery. In this piece, Galsworthy shows his admiration for those men who gallantly act to protect and serve the opposite sex regardless of the cost to themselves.

In *A Man of Devon,* Galsworthy struggled to find a personal voice as a short-story writer. In three of the four stories he used someone else's. In "The Salvation of Swithin Forsyte" he found his own.

A Commentary (1908)

A Commentary is a book of twenty short, satirical sketches in which Galsworthy presents contemporary problems and the realities of life in an industrial society to an audience of readers not much given to thinking about the poor, the unemployed, the aged, and the powerless. Galsworthy indicts the economic system of Edwardian England, and asks, "What will we do about it?"

A crippled old man whose job is to warn the public of the danger of a steam roller points out the evils of society as an introduction to the commentary provided in the sketches. "A Lost Dog" shows how an unemployed man can come to think of himself as an animal. "Demos" portrays a brutal man who cannot accept that his wife has left him for good reasons: "I'm 'er 'usband, an I mean to 'ave er, alive or dead."[5]

In "Old Age," a seventy-one-year-old painter, out of work, with no food or blankets, and his equally old wife refuse to go into a workhouse for the poor. "The Careful Man" satirizes a politician afraid that social change will take place too quickly. "Facts" satirizes the literal-minded. "Fear" depicts the terror of an unemployed and dying consumptive who is no longer able to support his family. In "Fashion," Galsworthy attacks insensitive rich women, as he would do in the novel *Fraternity*. Fashion is allegorized as an elegant lady: "You pass, glittering . . . and the eyes of the hollow-chested work girls on the pavement fix on you a thousand eager looks. . . . They do not know that you are as dead as snow around a crater" (*C,* 97).

"Sport" depicts the harassment of a prostitute. "Money" points out the idolatrous worship of wealth. "Progress" shows that modern inventions do not serve the progress of humanity. Other pieces show the barriers middle-class society erects to protect itself from those aspiring to rise out of poverty. In "Justice" the author argues, as he does on the stage, that there is one law for the rich and another for the poor. "Mother" and "Child" depict the effect of poverty on the helpless. But at the end, "Hope" somewhat sentimentally indicates that optimism can survive even in an old cripple, if courage endures.

As always, Galsworthy's heart is in the right place. However well-meaning, the viewpoint is still that of a rich reformer venturing from his club to observe and deplore. The sketches are frank, uncomplicated, and only a little self-conscious, but they lack individuality. That is their fatal weakness. One at a time they have some impact. All together they cancel each other out.

A Motley (1910)

A Motley is a collection of twenty-eight stories, studies, and impressions written between 1899 and 1910, many of which first appeared in such periodicals as the *English Review, Nation, English-*

woman, and *Westminster Gazette.* The book opens with a sketch that is obviously a portrait of, and a homage to, the author's solicitor father at age eighty. "A Portrait" had not been previously published. Galsworthy saved it for a place of honor in this collection. His painting of his deceased father is most tender and loving. The author also seems to be intending to show the source of his own convictions and carings, for the unnamed old gentleman believed that "money was . . . the symbol of a well-spent, well-ordered life."[6] He had "never been a sportsman—not being in the way of hunting . . . preferring to spend such time as he might have had for shooting, in communing with his beloved mountains" (*M,* 10). His "love of beauty was a sensuous, warm glow, secretly separating him from the majority of his associates" (*M,* 10). The old man believed in equality, saw charity as a personal obligation, and loved cricket. Furthermore, he did not like the profession of law. Galsworthy was reminding himself that the apple does not fall far from the tree.

"A Fisher of Men" is a short story, a portrait, and a study all in one. In this piece Galsworthy depicts a country parson who feels that his congregation does not give him his due. His flock constantly diminished during his twenty years of pastoring, for he was small-minded: "His face had been set, too, against irreverence; no one . . . might come to his church in flannel trousers" (*M,* 33); and he was stiff-necked and without compassion, always pointing out that "the fearful and unbelieving shall have their part in the lake which burneth fire and brimstone" (*M,* 33). He has no love or gentleness for his parishioners. Vexed near to madness by their rejection, he prays himself to death in a fierce rain by the seashore and they bury him beneath a paradoxically admonishing and forgiving inscription: "God is love" (*M,* 49). As usual, Galsworthy is hard on the established church and its purveyors of religion. Their intolerance of human drives and needs is not only counterproductive, it is a repressive source of human unhappiness. "A Fisher of Men" is one of Galsworthy's finest stories to the time he penned it, 1908. The parson is a tragic, Captain Ahab–like figure. The author's treatment of him is a skillful mix of invective, satire, and sharp characterization.

"The Prisoner" is a story full of compassion and pathos, in which Galsworthy shows the dehumanizing effect of long imprisonment. He argues that no crime committed by a human is equal to the crime done to that person by the state when it incarcerates him or her for tens of years or even life. Galsworthy's horror of imprisonment in small cells seems almost claustrophobic.

In "A Parting," the persona observes and comments on the farewell of a pair of lovers. It contrasts with the lightly ironic depiction of two lovers having their first secret meeting presented earlier in *A Motley* as "The Meeting." "The Japanese Quince" is a charming vignette in which a flowering exotic tree attracts two very conservative business men, who, although next-door neighbors, have never spoken to each other. The tree almost brings them together, but alas, their inbred reticence prevents friendship for these mirror-image men, and they return to relating to life through their newspapers.

"The Consummation," a rare, lighter moment in Galsworthy's stories, is an amusing piece for any reader familiar with Galsworthy's life. An amiable man named Harrison is told at a railway station by a lady in whom he is interested: "Why don't you write? You are just the person!" (*M*, 223). This, of course, is what Ada had said to Galsworthy to get him started on a career. Harrison writes a collection of short stories that he can only get published by subsidizing it. It receives good reviews, however, and he is compared to Poe, de Maupassant, and Kipling. Harrison decides to write a novel, and a friend who is "a man of genius" (*M*, 225) undertakes to "help" him. As a result, the novel is less well received by the public but is admired by the "man of genius." Then a well-known critic decides to help him make "art" out of his work. Each new book is less well received by the public and more difficult to read, but to the critical eye his work is advancing. Finally, Harrison writes a novel that is truly great: " 'I *have* done it at last. It *is good,* wonderfully good!' . . . He had indeed exhausted his public. It was *too* good—he could not read it himself! Returning to his cottage he placed the manuscript in the drawer. He never wrote another word" (*M*, 233). The man of genius is Joseph Conrad and the critic is Edward Garnett, and Galsworthy is getting even, good-naturedly, for the early somewhat insincere patronizing by the former and the school-mastering of the latter, both trying to make Galsworthy a "serious" writer. In truth Galsworthy was always content in being a middle-brow writer for a middle-brow audience.

"Once More" is a powerful and moving story of a young flower girl, resembling Mrs. Megan in the play *The Pigeon,* who, deserted by her young husband, attempts prostitution to support her child. In the end he returns, starving and frozen, and she takes him back into her arms to nurture him.

A Motley shows growth in narrative skills. Galsworthy was learning how to trim back the elaborate plots of *A Man of Devon* and expand on the acute economical character insights of *A Commentary*. Combining simple and believable plots with sharp observation and a less self-conscious prose style would result in the master story-telling evidenced in the later collections.

The Little Man (1915)

The Little Man contains a short play with the same title; a second entitled *Hall-Marked;* ten satiric sketches of such contemporary types as "The Writer," "The Critic," "The Plain Man," "The Artist," "The Housewife," and "The Competitor," generally shown as selfish, egotistical, competitive, and argumentative; and nine short stories of which "The Voice of_____," "A Simple Tale," and "Ultima Thule" are the best known and most memorable.

"The Voice of_____" takes place in a music hall where the program has become rather sordid, featuring a woman dancing indecorously. A voice is heard condemning the performance, and a strange light is seen on stage. The audience departs in terror and the theater staff are perplexed. The implication is that the voice of God has cried out against the profanation of female beauty.

"A Simple Tale" uses Ferrand again to comment on how the poor are neglected. In it a demented old man who thinks he is the Wandering Jew of ancient legend becomes more Chirst-like as he endures suffering and neglect. Indirectly, it is also an attack on anti-Semitism.

The last piece in *The Little Man*, "Ultima Thule," is a touching story of an old musician who feeds stray cats and mends injured birds instead of feeding himself. He dies and his beloved bullfinch falls dead on his heart. The old man is a St. Francis of Assisi, and the story is one of Galsworthy's many tributes to humans who love and save animals. In death "his face, as white now, almost as his silvery head, had in the sunlight a radiance like that of a small, bright angel gone to sleep."[7]

The Little Man is not a major part of Galsworthy's short fiction. In one or two stories, however, it foreshadows the achievements of *Five Tales* and *Captures*.

Five Tales (1918)

In *Five Tales* Galsworthy reaches the height of his ability as a writer of short stories. Two of these tales, "A Stoic" and "The Apple Tree," are his most anthologized stories. "Indian Summer of a Forsyte" not only serves as a bridge between *The Man of Property* and the rest of the *Saga,* it is the single most lyric moment in the entire chronicles. Although "The First and the Last" was begun just before the war, the five stories were a product of the First World War, but only the shortest, "The Juryman," deals with the conflict. Galsworthy used the writing of these long stories as a method of escaping from dismal reality into the happier world of the imagination, and in the case of "The Apple Tree," particularly, the world of love, beauty, and interpersonal passion.

"The First and the Last" is a melodramatic tale of passion, murder, and suicide, in which an eminent but ruthless attorney tries to conceal the crime of his weak but kindly younger brother. The latter has killed a brute who was forcing his attentions on the devoted young prostitute with whom the young man is having an affair. The older brother is motivated to help, not out of love, but out of a desire to protect his own reputation. Thus, when an innocent tramp is accused and sentenced to death, the attorney is delighted, and plans to send the lovers to Argentina. But the younger brother has too much integrity and compassion to allow someone else to die for his crime. The lovers choose suicide, leaving an exonerating note. But when the attorney finds the bodies, he destroys the note to save himself, even though it means an innocent man will die. Thus, the powerful older brother, first in the world, becomes last in the eyes of God, while the poor, lowly lovers have become first.

The story's ending is tragically ironic. The lovers' sacrifice has been for naught. In this world at least, the hard ones, without principles, triumph. Galsworthy turned this story into an effective one-act play. In both story and play he is especially skillful in delineating the character of Wanda, the Polish-born prostitute. She is a touching figure of female helplessness, a young woman who, despite being the victim of male exploitation and domination, maintains her great innate capacity for love, devotion, and abnegation.

"A Stoic" takes place in Liverpool in 1905. As with "The First and the Last" and also "The Apple Tree," Galsworthy turned the story into a play, in this case a three-act comedy called *Old English.* Again Galsworthy draws a vivid and memorable old man, Sylvanus Heythorp, an unscrupulous company director who lives life to the full. He is the father of an illegitimate son by a mistress who has died, and he has also fathered two legitimate children by an unloved wife, also deceased. For some years he has been a widower doting on the family of his illegitimate son, whom he loved most of all but who died young and impoverished.

Old Heythorp goes deeply into debt to support his life-style, and in order to obtain cash, he carries out an unlicensed transaction for a large commission. Trapped by a hating creditor trying to disgrace him just before death, the eighty-year-old Heythorp shows his disdain for his enemies and society by ending his life with a glorious dinner deliciously described by Galsworthy. He literally eats, drinks, and smokes himself into a happy sleep from which he does not awake. The author and the reader identify with the old bon vivant and his joie de vivre. He successfully defied society's conventions and got away with it.

"The Apple Tree" is the perennially favorite story of Galsworthy fans. Based on an old Dartmoor legend of a girl crossed in love who takes her own life, it is his most finely crafted, most symbolic, and most poetic tale.[8] The title is from a line of Gilbert Murray's translation of Euripides' play *Hippolytus:* "The apple tree, the singing and the gold," a line Galsworthy uses to open and close the story.

The simple plot centers on the return of Frank Ashurst, a middle-aged man, to the place on the moorlands of Devonshire where, twenty-six years ago, as a twenty-three-year-old student, he met, made love to, proposed to, and abandoned a beautiful, seventeen-year-old Welsh farm girl named Megan. After recalling the memory, he learns that she drowned herself after he deserted her. Ashurst, his life turned to ashes by the revelation, believes that he has been punished by love for his traitorous ways: " 'The Cyprian,' goddess of love [had] taken her revenge! And before his eyes, dim with tears, came Megan's face with the sprig of apple blossoms in her dark wet hair."[9]

Galsworthy symbolically evokes memories of both the Garden of Eden, with its apple of temptation, and the Garden of the Hesperides, with its golden apples, the prizes for great efforts.[10] Frank finds Megan beneath an apple tree in a garden. She is both an Aphrodite and an Eve. He rejects the goddess of love by mistaking her for the temptress, and by marrying Stella, a figure like the Artemis of *Hippolytus* and Diana, the goddess of chastity and the night. In doing so, and because he is prideful and unable to embrace the primordial patterns of life, Frank loses the garden for both of them. Megan dies, and he lives a sterile and conventional life. All that remains for him is the memory that once "he was not quite sane, thinking of that morning's kiss, and of tonight under the apple tree [where] fauns and dryads surely lived" (*FT,* 219).

"The Juryman" is the story of Henry Bosengate, a successful businessman, who during the First World War is called upon to serve on a jury hearing the case of an army private who was so miserable away from his wife that he tried to kill himself. He is charged with attempting suicide and thus trying to deprive the king of a soldier. Bosengate finds his sympathy growing for the accused, and he argues successfully on his behalf with the other jurors. Returning home after the trial, he realizes how much he loves and needs his wife, Kate, whom he has taken for granted. He thinks: "We haven't been close— really close, you and I, so that we each understand what the other is feeling. It's all in that, you know; understanding—sympathy—it's priceless. When I saw that poor devil . . . sent back to his regiment to begin his sorrows all over again—wanting his wife, thinking and thinking of her just as you know I'd be thinking and wanting you, I thought what an awful outside sort of life we lead, never telling each other what we really think and feel, never being really close" (*FT,* 281).

The sensitive tale proposes that there is a store of warmth and compassion in most people. One can learn from the misfortune and suffering of another that the time to cherish those one loves is now.

The beautiful "Indian Summer of a Forsyte," discussed in chapter 3, is the last story in *Five Tales.* These long pieces, especially "The Apple Tree," "A Stoic" and "Indian Summer of a Forsyte," show Galsworthy's mastery of the genre. His short fiction could create that kind of resonance in a reader that causes him or her to go back to the piece again and again to find new meaning, as well as remembered beauty.

Tatterdemalion (1920)

The last of Galsworthy's war stories and the first of his stories written in the peace that followed appeared in *Tatterdemalion,* a "ragamuffin" of a collection. The book contains fifteen pieces in "Part I. Of War-time" and eight in "Part II. Of Peace-time." All are shorter than the stories in *Five Tales,* and they are not memorable, representing Galsworthy's lesser fictional efforts of the 1914–19 period. The stories are generally about the fate of the noncombatants on the home front in the war, the unsung sacrifice of some, and the unnecessary suffering of others at the hands of jingoists.

The first story, "The Grey Angel," is probably a companion piece to "Portrait" in *A Motley*, in that it seems to be a fictionalized and idealized sketch of his mother, who died in 1915. In it a valiant eighty-year-old English lady gives her all doing Red Cross work in France during the war. She thinks of everyone but herself, and although most of the gifts she brings the wounded French soldiers are useless to them, they appreciate the spirit of heartfelt giving. As she dies, she shows her inner peace, her indifference to death, and her concern for her children: " 'My darlings—don't cry; smile!'"[11]

"Defeat" tells of a German prostitute trapped in London during the war and, in order to survive, forced to service the very soldiers who are killing her countrymen in battle. Her life is, to Galsworthy, as terrible as any combatant's. In fact, the wounded young officer she picks up enjoys trench warfare: "It was great. We did laugh that morning. They got me much too soon, though—a swindle!" (*T*, 45). He had been cut down in a charge by four machine-gun bullets. Galsworthy was naive and out of touch in implying, as late as 1916, the date of the writing of the story, that most English soldiers were exhilarated by battle. The poor girl suffers terribly as she hears of an English victory and then tears up the money the soldier gave her. Alone, lying on the floor, she sings *"Die Wacht am Rhein"* (*T*, 49).

"Flotsam and Jetsam," "Cafard," and "Bidan" are stories about wounded French soldiers and stem from Galsworthy's hospital experience. "The Recruit" is about an undersized Dartmoor agricultural worker of little intelligence who tries to enlist but is rejected. He is deeply hurt, but of course, he survives the war while the brighter and stronger die by the millions. "The Peace Meeting" tells of an attempt to end the war that is frustrated by the very men it could save. In "Heaven and Earth" an old man sadly buries his dog, ironically noting that he could be sad for an animal's death and impervious to the war slaughter. In "The Muffled Ship" Canadian soldiers return home. "Heritage" tells of the service to crippled children and those who were air-raid victims. "The Mother Stone" implies that the First World War occurred because of the greed and power-seeking of colonial exploiters. "The Bright Side" and "The Dog It Was That Died" attack the British treatment of resident Germans, like Galsworthy's brother-in-law, during the war years, while "Recorded" is a soldier's sad farewell to his wife and babes. "A Green Hill Far Away" is a thanksgiving for peace.

"Part II. Of Peace-time" begins with an excellent tale, "Spindle-berries," one of Galsworthy's finest short stories. It tells of two paint-ers, cousins: a woman who gives up everything for beauty, and a man who is commercially successful and who is both disdainful and jealous of his relative. "Life! Alica! She had made a pretty mess of it, and yet who knew what secret raptures she had felt with her subtle lover, beauty, by starlight and sunlight and moonlight, in the fields and woods, on the hilltops, and by riverside! . . . Who could say that she had missed the prize of life?" (T, 224–25).

"Expectations" is a somewhat humorous story of a married couple inept in everything except keeping their relationship going. "Manna" is a biting tale of the travails of a stubborn clergyman, reminiscent of Reverend Pierson in Saint's Progress. "Two Looks" tells of the pain-ful love of two women for the same dying old man. "Fairyland" is a very short but lovely countryside sketch. "A Strange Thing," "The Nightmare Child," and "Buttercup-night" are village tales set in a place like Manaton on Dartmoor.

Tatterdemalion is a minor work. As much as anything it is a work-book for themes, ideas, and scenes in the novels and plays written during the same period. Captures comes much closer to the great skill in writing short fiction Galsworthy showed in Five Tales.

Captures (1923)

Captures contains sixteen short stories. The first, longest, and strongest is "A Feud." Another Dartmoor piece like "The Apple Tree," it is a village tragedy in which two men quarrel over the shooting of a dog, engage in a disastrous law suit, and cause the death of one litigant's son, who runs off to the war. In the end, the young man's contentious father, while trying to kill his enemy, hears the church bell tolling for his son's death, and "in Bowden something went out. He had not the heart to hate."[12] It has taken the death of a loved one to bring peace to two troubled families. In "A Feud," Galsworthy again shows that he can write with success about rural, agricultural people. Of course in his home at Manaton he had direct daily contact with them. Galsworthy had less success depicting the proletariat and urban poor, for although he had great sympathy for them, he had almost no contact with them.

In "Timber," a baronet decides to sell his ancestral works to the government during the war to make great profit and appear patriotic at the same time. Walking in the woods in winter, he loses his way and freezes to death. The woods take revenge before their own demise. "Santa Lucia," "Blackmail," "A Hedonist," "Stroke of Lightning," and "A Long-ago Affair" are effective stories of sexual passion, longing, and jealousy concerning middle-aged spouses and lovers. "The Broken Boot" and "The Man Who Kept His Form" are sad pieces about men who struggle to live up to a code of honor and a way of life. In the former it is an impoverished actor and in the latter a gentleman, the dying "symbol of that lost cause, gentility" (*CAP*, 74).

"Philanthropy" and "Acme" are stories of writers who are surprised by the unexpected ways of their fellow humans. "Salta pro Nobis (A Variation)" is a version of the Mata Hari story: a dancer spy performs for the last time before being shot. "Late—299," like the play *Justice*, shows the devastating result of imprisonment. A doctor serves two years for performing an abortion on a woman to save her honor. Afterward, with anger and cynicism, he defies the world: "I am so human that I'll see the world damned before I'll take its pity. . . . Leave me alone. I am content" (*CAP*, 265). "Conscience" and "Virtue" show young men who act according to their conscience regardless of personal cost.

"Had a Horse," the last and second longest story in *Captures* tells of a nonentity of a bookmaker who obtains a racehorse as payment on a debt and for the first time actually sees such an animal. He comes to love the beauty of his beast, and his regard for his animal gives him pride and self-respect that lasts "for years betting on horses he never saw, underground like a rat, yet never again so accessible to the kicks of fortune, or so prone before the shafts of superiority" (*CAP*, 306). In this story Galsworthy enjoys showing his intimate and precise knowledge of the sport of kings.

In *Captures* Galsworthy once more approaches the level of excellence in short fiction first achieved in *Five Tales*. Galsworthy's post–World War I outlook, however, was different from that he espoused during fierce wartime. His fiction mellowed, grew more nostalgic, and showed a growing tolerance for human frailty.

From *A Man of Devon* through *Captures*, Galsworthy's short fiction paralleled his novels in subject and style. His ability as a novelist peaked first, before the First World War, with the social satires like

A *Man of Property* and *The Country House*. The high-water mark of his
short fiction came later, during the war, with *Five Tales*. When he
continued the chronicles after the war, his interest in the short story
declined.

Although produced by a master stylist, a skilled satirist, and a
careful craftsman, Galsworthy's short fiction has several imperfections. For one, the author is often a blatant sentimentalist, particularly when it comes to portraying women or the poor. His women are
almost always self-sacrificing sufferers like Wanda, the Polish prostitute in "The First and the Last," May, the German prostitute in "Defeat," or Megan in "The Apple Tree." They are invariably courageous
in their travail, like Mrs. Holsteig in "The Dog It Was That Died,"
the Scotswoman whose German-born husband and English-born son
are interned in the war. When old, like the "Grey Angel" they are
noble. Galsworthy's chivalric code seems to have made him incapable
of villainizing a woman or granting her major human imperfections,
at least within the confines of short fiction.

Also, Galsworthy's working-class men, like Tom in "The Recruit"
and the private in "The Juryman," are almost always humble hat-in-
handers. They are primitively eloquent, but ultimately unconvincing
in dialogue or dialect.

Other characters bathe in self-pity. Sometimes, particularly in the
fine depiction of old men like Heythorp in "A Stoic," there is "at
times the breath of decadence."[13] These men fear death less because
of a natural terror of oblivion or concern for an afterlife, than because
their already dulling senses will be forever extinguished.

Finally, Galsworthy's stories are unrelentingly serious. Humor is
almost totally absent. An occasional lighter touch would have offered
a contrast that could have exculpated the author from the charges of
bleakness and unremitting pessimism.

Still, on balance, few of Galsworthy's contemporaries spoke out in
short fiction against the injustice of life as successfully as he did. Nor
did they match his broad vision of an often hypocritical society in
transition from the seemingly stable Victorian era to the war-weary,
cynical, anarchistic, and sexually emancipated world of the 1920s.

Chapter Seven
The Playwright of Conscience

John Galsworthy struggled nine years for recognition as a fiction writer. Fame as a dramatist came far more easily, perhaps too easily, with the production of his first completed full-length play, *The Silver Box* (1906).[1] In 1923 the critic William Archer could say with confidence that "Mr. Galsworthy raises no critical problems like those presented by Mr. Shaw and Mr. Barker. He has written three of the finest plays of our time—*The Silver Box, Strife,* and *Justice.* . . . He writes with quiet, easy mastery, telling . . . a quiet simple story which enables him to contrast two social strata . . . without any didactic emphasis."[2]

Writing three years after Galsworthy's death, Ford Madox (Hueffer) Ford opined that his friend's "temporal success as novelist obscured his much greater artistic achievement with the drama. . . . [His] dogged determination to present antitheses . . . was exactly suited to the theatre. . . . Galsworthy picks up every crumb of interest and squeezes the last drop of drama out of a situation."[3]

Few critics today are as sanguine about Galsworthy's contribution and worth as a dramatist. Perhaps close to the truth is John Gassner's evaluation of Galsworthy the dramatist as a "technician," who contributed "interest, charm, and power to the theatre . . . but did not rock it to its foundations."[4] Still, in his own lifetime Galsworthy was second only to Shaw on the English stage, and he was considered the chief English inheritor of Ibsenism. He took the problem play from Ibsen, simplified it, and divested it of preaching and propaganda. Through strong characterizations, tightly constructed naturalistic plots, and vivid dialogue, he attacked most of the social problems of his time: the unfair justice system, the repression of women in family and society, tensions between parents and children, exploitation of labor, anti-Semitism, poverty, strikes, jingoism, and others.

Galsworthy wrote twenty-two full-length plays and many short plays, a few of which are closet pieces and others dramatizations of stories. His dramatic technique seldom varies. He presents a near-balanced view of the play's problem or thesis through a highly dramatic situation supported by extremely realistic dialogue, seemingly uncontrived and nonpoetic and thus considered radical in its day. The denouement is left partially open and tinged with irony because Galsworthy sees a play, like life itself, more prone to questions than to answers. He eschews the deus ex machina ending for neatness's sake or the contrived finales of "the well-made play."

Surely Galsworthy's major contribution to the English theater is that he helped orchestrate the revolt against the tradition of melodrama on the stage that had tyrannized playwrights since the nineteenth century. Working together, Shaw, Galsworthy, and the writer-director-manager Harley Granville Barker established realism, naturalism, and social consciousness as the norms in both text and performance on the English stage, leading a parade of realistic critical playwrights that ends in John Osborne and Arnold Wesker. Even the naturalistic stage settings of Harold Pinter's plays stem from those of the early pioneers of English Ibsenism.

The major plays of John Galsworthy are *The Silver Box* (1906), *Strife* (1909), *Justice* (1910), *The Pigeon* (1912), *The Eldest Son* (1912), *The Fugitive* (1913), *The Mob* (1914), *The Skin Game* (1920), *Loyalties* (1922), and *Escape* (1926). Galsworthy first attempted to write drama in 1901 with an unfinished play titled "The Civilized." In it a Forsyte woman attempts to escape from an unhappy marriage through a love affair with the brother of her best friend. The lover has died, but the husband finds out about the affair and threatens divorce. The wife, like Nora in *A Doll's House,* walks out on him. Marital problems, family strife, and divorce would remain a staple of Galsworthy's plots.

The Silver Box

Galsworthy's first produced play immediately established the author as a major British playwright. He maintained that position throughout his lifetime, even though his reputation as a dramatist began to decline after the First World War.[5] *The Silver Box* was the result of only a few weeks work on Galsworthy's part, urged by Edward Garnett who felt that his friend should contribute to the Vedrenne-Barker management scheme of introducing important writers to the theater.[6]

The Silver Box, first titled "The Cigarette Box," dramatizes the inequities of the English system of justice. In it two men steal. Jack

Barthwick, son of a wealthy Liberal member of Parliament, on a whim steals a handbag with a purse in it from a prostitute with whom he has spent the evening. Jim Jones, unemployed husband of the elder Barthwick's charwoman, steals a cigarette box and the already once-stolen purse. The prostitute threatens prosecution, and the elder Barthwick tries to bribe her off to keep the affair out of the newspapers. He also suspects Mrs. Jones of stealing. The poor woman is terribly frightened. The case goes to trial, and in a London police court it is soon proved who really took the silver box. Jones goes to prison, while young Barthwick, with the aid of expensive attorneys gets off scot free. The senior Barthwick's liberalism is proved superficial when his self interests are threatened. When at the end of the play, having lost her job, the charwoman turns to her former employer in supplication, he can only slink away, his hypocrisy unmasked. Mrs. Jones, innocent of everything, suffers most of all, while Jim Jones speaks the moral of the play: "Call this justice? What about 'im? E got drunk! E took the purse . . . but . . . it's 'is money got 'im off—*Justice!*"[7]

In *The Silver Box,* Galsworthy introduced a technique he would use throughout his career as a playwright, that of dramatic contrast. Character, situations, and settings are present in parallel.[8] Here the rich son and the poor son, the rich parent and the poor parent, the wealthy home and the impoverished home allow audience comparison and judgment. Galsworthy saw the dramatist as a "scientist" presenting "the social fabric" as evidence without requiring direct comment.[9] Thus Galsworthy avoids propaganda and melodrama. Ordinary people go about their business in reasonable and natural ways. Critics generally have admired this clarity of presentment, which William York Tyndall calls a "monolithic simplicity of treatment."[10]

Strife

When first performed, *Strife* was a "spectacle" that "many could not witness . . . dry-eyed."[11] It is one of the important early dramas depicting the conflict between capital and labor and is somewhat reminiscent of Gerhart Hauptmann's *The Weavers* (1892). Written prior the great strike of 1911 and the General Strike of 1926, it did not record British industrial history; it foretold it.

In *Strife,* two protagonists, firebrand David Roberts, a union leader, and old and obstinate John Anthony, chairman of the board of the Trenartha Tin Plate Works, fall, like hubristic Greek heroes, due to the backsliding and disaffecting of their followers, whom they have outdistanced in their fury, violence, and anger. In the end the audience admires them both and sympathizes with the fallen leaders, who, indeed, come to respect each other.

The play's action covers only a few hours. The company board meets to try to end the strike. Neither Roberts nor Anthony will compromise or give in. Separate meetings of the workers and the owners, and the labor-management confrontations present the usual Galsworthy parallelism and balance in the play's structure. In the end, compromise wins out at the cost of the power of the two protagonists, but only after there has been suffering and death.

Strife, although ostensibly concerned with the cruelties and hardships caused by industrial conflict, is really about pride and power. Galsworthy said, "In *Strife* the fatal thing is strong will minus self-control and balance."[12] Roberts and Anthony are strong but blinded by their convictions, and like so many political heroes who fail, "they are snowed under by the sheer weight of mediocrity."[13]

Ultimately, in *Strife* Galsworthy cries out that the victims of power struggles must be remembered, that great disputes are more often due to the intransigence of leaders than the beliefs or desires of followers, and that extremism wreaks havoc in society, which must be based on tolerance, comity, and good will.

Justice

Galsworthy was always horrified, almost traumatized, by the thought of incarceration. *Justice* allowed the author to vent his hatred for the mental torture, the physical degradation, and the moral disintegration that punishment brings during and after imprisonment. The play's title is ironic. Formal justice is not just. As the defense attorney states in court, "Justice is a machine that, when someone has once given it the starting push, rolls on of itself" (*PL,* 153).

In *Justice,* a young man named Falder is discovered to have forged a check. He intended to use the money to go abroad with the woman he loves, a married woman who has been mistreated by her brutal husband. Refusing to be merciful, Falder's employer, the solicitor James How, turns him in to the police, and the machinery of justice begins to move inexorably. The superb trial scene has the defense attorney pleading for understanding for a gentle but weak person emotionally distressed by the cruel treatment of his lover. But the prosecution, judge, and jury are prejudiced because Falder loves a married woman, even though the two have not committed adultery. Falder is found guilty of forgery and sentenced to three years in prison.

In prison, Falder must routinely spend three months in solitary confinement, during which time the monotony and loneliness nearly drive him mad. In the final scene of the third act, Falder is driven to flinging himself at the cell door and beating on it in desperation. In the fourth and last act he has been released, and trying to get his position back with Mr. How, he runs up against hard-heartedness toward a "gaol-bird" and all "weak characters." How will give Falder another chance if he is willing to give up his lover, who meanwhile has separated from her husband. But Falder cannot bear to give up the only person who has cared for him and forges a reference in order to obtain another job. Failing to report for police supervision and about to be rearrested, Falder cannot face the thought of a return to prison hell and flings himself over the stairs, breaking his neck.

Like *The Silver Box*, *Justice* shows the implacable folly and unfairness of the legal system. Moreover, it also exposes without sentimentality the great social cost of that system. Furthermore, *The Silver Box*, *Justice*, and *Strife* delineate the conflict that individuals often have to engage in against frozen ideas and the institutions that support them.

Dramaturgically, Galsworthy from the beginning shows his ability to present realistic social themes in a naturalistic theatrical setting. With *Justice*, however, the playwright also indicates skill in simultaneously presenting both social and domestic themes. Falder's crime and his love affair are both individually explicated and successfully integrated in a deterministic action. Although the play cannot reflect the intense experience of a Jean Genet, a Brendan Behan, or a Miguel Piñero, it was convincing enough to help effect changes in the British prison system.

The Pigeon

The Pigeon asks, if once social deterioration has taken place and humans have been reduced to poverty and degradation, can the forces that attempted to destroy them be reversed by individual humanitarianism, so that the seemingly lost people of the underclass can be reclaimed? Conceived as a fantasy, the play tells the story of Christopher Wellwyn, an amiable middle-aged artist, who lives with his daughter Ann and who loves humankind so much that he continually gives his substance to anyone who can move him with a pathetic tale. Ann is convinced that the recipients of her father's generosity are unworthy of it, and she is usually right, but he cannot help but love his fleecers. Appearing again in a Galsworthy work, Ferrand identifies Wellwyn as the "poor pigeon" of the title (*PL,* 196). He also states that he and others have been taken care of by "an angel!" (*PL,* 197). For Wellwyn is like a St. Cristopher, a bearer of Christ.

In the end Wellwyn proves to be ineffectual. His desire to aid humankind is defeated by the individuality and obstinacy of people, the very people he desires to aid. Still, his efforts are courageous and commendable, even though the moral of the play is that real help and meaningful change may be impossible given human nature.

Galsworthy's characterization in *The Pigeon* is particularly fine. He is more convincing in creating images of the poor and indigent in drama than he is in fiction. Timson, the old horsecab driver, is a wonderful portrait of a crafty sponger, and the young flower girl, Mrs. Megan, who goes out on the streets, and then tries to drown herself, is yet another of the excellent portraits in *The Pigeon.* Moreover, the language of *The Pigeon* is more imagistic and lyric than Galsworthy's usual precise, almost metallic dialogue.

The Eldest Son

The Eldest Son was writen just before *Justice,* but not produced until after *The Pigeon.*[14] As in *The Silver Box,* it is revealed that there is one set of rules for the rich and another, more strict, for the poor. Bill, the eldest son of Sir William Cheshire, has impregnated the maid, Freda Studdenham, but the family is unaware of this fact early in the play when they meet to discuss the village gossip about a girl who has been made pregnant by a young worker on the Cheshire estate. Sir William has forced the young man to propose marriage to the girl on threat of expulsion from job and home. Then Bill and Freda are caught together, and Bill states that he intends to marry the maid. The marriage must be prevented at all costs. Sir William hypocritically reverses his moral judgments of the previous evening when it comes to the future of his son and heir. Sir William attempts to draw off Freda, but he is an English gentleman and is unable to threaten or cajole her. Instead, he turns to Bill and warns his son that if he marries Freda he must then on fend for himself as he will be disinherited. But Freda saves him; she will accept no charity marriage that can only lead to a lifetime of unhappiness. Although the Cheshires are relieved, the moral victory belongs to Freda and her worker father. Yet it is clear from the parallel relationships that the aristocrats get off while the workers pay for their mistakes and are forced to meet their obligations.

The Eldest Son is less didactic than *The Silver Box,* but it is also less theatrically effective. Its great strength is in an almost Chekhov-like depiction of a family of country aristocracy with a saintly mother, a John Bull of a father, and a believable collection of sons and daughters, servants and caretakers. It is the latter, the workingfolk, who foil the Forsyte-like caste intolerance and abject self-serving of the rich. Galsworthy's target here is the blatant control and manipulation of the powerful over the weak, as succinctly expressed by Sir William: "Unless we're true to our caste, and prepared to work for it, the landed classes are going to go under to this infernal democratic spirit in the air" (*PL,* 117). Galsworthy's attitude toward the landed aristocracy will change after World War I, but *The Eldest Son* is still the product of the conscience behind the writing of Galsworthy's novels of social satire.

The Fugitive

The Fugitive depicts a woman's flight from an unhappy marriage to her eventual suicide. Clare Dedmond is a dramatic version of Irene in *A Man of Property*. Like other protagonists in Galsworthy's plays and novels, she is in conflict with society. She has married young and inexperienced, and her husband, George, is without much wit or imagination. He has money; Clare has charm. She does not love her husband but has too great a sense of honor to betray him. Finally, she comes under the influence of a writer, Kenneth Malise, and she tells her husband that she wishes to leave him. George responds by forcibly taking her. She leaves him and goes to Malise for advice, but George has him followed by detectives looking for evidence for a divorce. Clare shrinks from her husband, but she also shrinks from the thought of a dishonorable affair with Malise, so she takes a job selling gloves in a shop. Unable to make a go of it she then becomes Malise's mistress. George offers to take her back but she refuses. In revenge,

George sues for divorce and demands damages from Malise, who first loses his position and then his feelings for Clare. Clare leaves him, falls into poverty, and considers prostitution. Despairing, she kills herself with sleeping pills in a last glass of champagne.

Clare Dedmond is one of the finest tragic women in all of modern English drama. In Galsworthy's time she was matched only by the heroine of Arthur Wing Pinero's *The Second Mrs. Tanqueray* (1893). Clare's decline and fall is both realistic and moving. Her inability to survive the change from an easy but empty life to a brutal but full one allows for a plot that illustrates Galsworthy's view of a true dramatic action: "what characters do, at once contrary, as it were, to expectation, and yet because they have done other things" (*IT*, 194).

The Mob

The Mob, reminiscent of Ibsen's *An Enemy of the People* (1882), is yet another Galsworthy play in which the individual is pitted against society. It is one of the author's most courageous works, written and produced just as war fever and anti-German sentiment were sweeping Britain, for in it the protagonist, Stephan More, under secretary of state and member of Parliament, fights against the deep convictions of his wife, his family, his friends, his constituents, the press, and the general public, in arguing that a great power like Britain must not oppress a smaller power, perhaps like the Boer Republic, although no small nation is mentioned.

More, like St. Thomas More, is an individualist with a strong conscience. Might does not make right for him. The dogs of war are not to be unleashed. But the war comes, and More devotes his life to an antiwar campaign. He is warned to flee the country, but he does not. His wife leaves him, and in the end he is killed by a mob. Just before dying he states his and Galsworthy's internationalist and humanitarian credo: "My country is not yours. Mine is that great country which shall never take toll from the weakness of others" (*PL*, 283).

Galsworthy was reacting to the growing jingoism in Britain in 1914. His cry for peace would shortly be drowned out along with so many other voices, including Shaw's and Bertrand Russell's, but it is to Galsworthy's undying credit that he sensed a great evil brewing and he tried to prevent it. The play is more melodramatic than most of Galsworthy's dramas, ending with a visual epilogue, the tombstone of More, inscribed: "Erected to the Memory of Stephen More. Faithful to his ideals" (*PL*, 273). Nevertheless, it is effective action drama, especially in the two mob scenes. Surprisingly well received in Britain, given the temper of the times, it received far greater acclaim in 1920 in New York.[15]

The Skin Game

The Skin Game, perhaps more than any other play by Galsworthy, has stood the test of time. The problem it concerns is archetypal, a feud between two families. The question is whether the newly rich Hornblowers should build a factory in a location that would completely ruin the view from the ancestral home of the Hillcrist family, landed gentry who have enjoyed their unspoiled ancestral surroundings for generations. Further complicating the situation is Mr. Hornblower's conviction that his wife has been snubbed by Mrs. Hillcrist, who later learns that the parvenu's daughter-in-law has a shady past and is able to blackmail Hornblower into reselling the property he planned to build on.

In *The Skin Game,* Galsworthy is arguing for reasonable behavior by both the nouveaux riches and the gentry. He wants people to try to settle problems amicably and to think before entering into feuds. No one comes off well in this drama except for a child of each family, who together unsuccessfully attempt to make peace.

The plot of this popular tragicomedy, Galsworthy's first great commercial success on the London stage, is suspenseful, with several exciting, melodramatic scenes, including a confrontation between a woman and the men in her shady past, and a suicide attempt. Written just after World War I ended, *The Skin Game* can also be read as an allegory on the war, with the respective families, intolerant, selfish, and intractable, representing the two sides in the recent conflict. In that postwar period, Galsworthy's finer plays, like *The Skin Game, Loyalties,* and *Escape,* were more skillfully constructed, but lacked some of the moral certitude and reforming zeal of the plays before the conflict—not necessarily a shortcoming. Along with *The Silver Box* and *Strife,* these later plays remain the most popular of Galsworthy's drama.

Loyalties

To his great credit, Galsworthy did not participate in the fashionable English upper-class and literary anti-Semitism prevalent in his time. Almost prescient of what would begin in Europe in the 1930s,

he spoke out against it, most eloquently and effectively in *Loyalties,*
where he attacks unwritten codes, misplaced loyalties, and vicious
prejudices "to stir up the audience, to make them reflect, to awake
in them a new perception and conscience, more humanitarian sentiments and deeper sympathy."[16] The play was a major success in Britain, America, and on the Continent.

In *Loyalties,* Ferdinand De Levis, a wealthy nouveau riche Jew and
another Galsworthy protagonist fighting alone against closed-ranked
society, is robbed of one thousand pounds while spending a weekend
with upper-class friends. He is quite sure that Captain Ronald Dancy,
who previously had given De Levis a racehorse with which he made
money, has broken into his room and taken the cash. He accuses
Dancy, and all of society rises to support the officer, cutting De Levis, driving him from his club, and ostracizing him from fashionable
society. Dancy sues De Levis for defamation of character after chal-
lenging him to a duel which De Levis refuses. It comes out in the
course of investigation that Dancy did steal the money in order to pay
off an old mistress. The court finds for De Levis, who tells Dancy that
he need not return the money nor pay costs, but finally the disgraced
officer shoots himself to death.

De Levis seeks justice. He is worldly enough to understand: "Society! Do you think I don't know that I'm only tolerated for my
money? Society can't add insult to injury and have my money as well"
(*PL,* 440). Most loyalties range against him: the personal loyalty of
gentlemen who cannot count a Jew among their number; social loyalty that places the good name of a club or a service over fairness; and
familial loyalty of loved ones supporting an erring family member.
On the other hand, it is De Levis's loyalty to his fellow religionists
that drives him on; and, finally, the law, Galsworthy's old profession,
is loyal to truth and justice. The latter more than balances all loyalties misplaced.

Characterization in *Loyalties* is powerful. Upper-class types are
swiftly and finely delineated, and De Levis is a Shylock without
meanness or villainy, while Dancy is an Antonio without honor.

Escape

In *Escape,* which Galsworthy intended to be his last play,[17] the
playwright eschews his usual three- or four-act structure in favor of
episodes. It contains ten episodes, including a prologue, depicting

Matt Denant's crime of manslaughter of a policeman, his escape from Dartmoor prison, and in his attempts to avoid recapture, his disguised meeting with various types of people who either help or hinder him. Finally, he takes sanctuarylike refuge in a country church. The parson is aware of Denant's presence, and when the convict's pursuers have tracked him to the vestry, the clergyman is about to lie to protect him, but he gives himself up to save the cleric's honor.

The play's title is ironic: no one escapes from life, the law, and most significantly for the play—himself. For Denant is a gentleman, something of a Forsyte type. In his travail he has learned that the qualities of charity, sympathy, integrity, and understanding are of more value than personal freedom. He finds the humanity that has remained submerged in his inner self and that is worth everything.

Escape is like a morality play. Denant is an Everyman, who makes mistakes, sins, and repents. He ends with a good deed, a sacrificial act that saves a fellow human. In that process he saves himself.

The black-and-white nature of *Escape*'s plot helped make *Escape* one of Galsworthy's major box-office successes.[18] It was also made into a film. Galsworthy's audience by this time expected, and always admired, his attack on the institutions of society that, in their rigidity, cause injustices and serve to encase, repress, and sometimes drown the human spirit. Although the strong Galsworthy social conscience may have wavered in the later novels, it remained, despite tempered rhetoric, untarnished and unvanquished in Galsworthy the playwright until the very end, his last piece of writing, the unfinished play *Similes*.[19]

Some of Galsworthy's other valued full-length dramas are *Joy* (1907), *A Bit O' Love* (1915), *Foundations* (1917), *A Family Man* (1921), *Windows* (1922), *The Forest* (1924), *Old English* (1924), *The Show* (1925), *Exiled* (1929), and *The Roof* (1929). Shorter plays by Galsworthy, particularly those based on his more well-known stories, remain a part of little-theater and school repertories.

Galsworthy, the humanitarian, used the drama for direct appeal to government and society for reform, understanding, and compassion. He spoke for the inarticulate of all classes. In the Manaton edition Galsworthy states: "It might be said of Shaw's plays that he creates characters who express feelings which they have not got. It might be said of mine, that I create characters who have feelings which they cannot express."[20] Although Galsworthy is being unkind to Shaw, he is accurate in his self-evaluation. His dramatic characters are seldom lyric. They more often move us with their fate rather than their words—just as in life. Furthermore, Galsworthy's purposeful noneloquence requires the actors in his plays to express meaning, significance, and truths through action, making for strong theater. In contrast, actors in Shaw plays often feel they are merely tape recorders for Shavian ideas.

Galsworthy's plays often have no villain. The great villain is society, usually personified by police or judges. his plays are full of irony and suspense, which produce a satisfying catharsis, for the audience departs feeling moved as well as satisfied. Sometimes, however, in attempting to educate and sway, Galsworthy sentimentalizes and even trivializes character and situation.

Finally, because John Galsworthy came to playwrighting impulsively and as a mature writer, he lacked the poetic vitality and the universality of his master, Ibsen, and the wit and dimension of his contemporary, Shaw. His drama, even at its best, is less subtle, and somewhat more dated, than his great social novels: *A Man of Property, The Country House, Fraternity,* and *The Patrician.* Furthermore, the theatrical impact of the new realism of Arthur Wing Pinero, Shaw, Harley Granville Barker, James M. Barrie, and Galsworthy has long since dissipated. In Galsworthy's case, there remains for the reader, and occasionally for the theatergoer, the passionate humanitarianism; the precise, historically interesting delineation of class distinction and prejudice; the bold, direct dramaturgy; and the high energy level of the dedicated playwright.

Chapter Eight
Poet and Essayist

John Galsworthy was nearly the complete man of letters, for besides his contributions as novelist, short-story writer, and playwright, he was also a poet, essayist, and critic. The latter endeavors do not add to his stature as a creative writer; nevertheless, in any attempt to comprehend fully the source, nature, and scope of Galsworthy's impact on British literature, they must be considered and evaluated.

Poetry

Galsworthy wrote some one hundred poems. Many were first published in such periodicals as *Atlantic Monthly, English Review, Nation,* and *Scribner's Magazine.* He loved poetry, continually polished his own verse, and wished for recognition as a poet, as well as a fiction writer and playwright. His protégé R. H. Mottram wryly notes: "There is almost a touch of comedy about the fact that the man who was destined to rank so high amid the novelists and playwrights of our history should have wished, if not all the time, fervently at many times, to be writing poetry. Such is the fact, plainly stated by him in letters to me."[1] Yet neither the critics nor the general reading public have taken to his conservative, old-fashioned, formal, personal, and sometimes esoteric verse, which he constantly revised, but which still contains instances of awkward phrasing, arbitrary inversions, words chosen for rhyme rather than sense, and pedestrian expression.

More than fiction or drama, poetry allowed Galsworthy simultaneously to satisfy several needs. First, it gave him the opportunity, sometimes also taken in the essay, to state directly a personal feeling or emotion. His fiction and drama are objective, and Galsworthy, stereotypically English, was not a demonstrative man personally. Second, poetry gave him an outlet for his lyric impulse, something he could share with a wife who was an accomplished musician and who wanted him to write songs she could set to music. Third, and most important, poetry was the medium through which Galsworthy expressed his philosophy and religion. In his youth Galsworthy rejected formal religion and orthodox Christianity. In his fiction he is either hostile to clerics or barely tolerant. It is in his poetry, however, that he admits to the existence of God and deals directly with the fundamental questions of the purpose of life and the accountability of human beings.

Moods, Songs, and Doggerels (1912). Containing fifty-eight pieces written over at least a seventeen-year period, *Moods, Songs, and Doggerels* documents Galsworthy's love of the land of his fathers in such works as: "Devon to Me!" "Gaulzery Moor," "Cuckoo Song: Dartmoor," "Land Song of the West Country," "Countryman's Song," "Village Sleep Song," "Drake's Spirit," "Plymouth," and "The Devon Sage." His affection for animals is expressed in "Magpie," about a sad bird always "lonely flying"; and "The Robin," which symbolizes nature's promise of regeneration:

> You are no bird, you fairy sprite
> In hue of red, and hue of dust,
> Who come to turn dark thoughts to light—
> For what are you but living trust?[2]

Of course, Galsworthy, the dog lover, includes an overly sentimental piece entitled "To My Dog," which includes some unfortunate lines like: "Then through the ages we'll retrieve / each other's scent and company" (*MSD*, 99).

Moods, Songs, and Doggerels, however, contains Galsworthy's longest and most philosophical poem, "A Dream," which back in 1901 he sent to Edward Garnett for criticism. Garnett, responding on 14 June was not encouraging. He felt that the poem was "altogether too *outré*. A meretricious method well worked out, would be my verdict. . . . I candidly own *the Dream* is clever—but I don't like its cleverness: it makes me feel old and prejudiced!"[3] Garnett does not seem to have given the poem an open-minded reading, but Galsworthy was very much under his influence at this early stage of his career, and so Garnett's response may have atrophied Galsworthy's confidence in himself as a poet.

Written in thirty-one eight-line stanzas of iambic tetrameter with an *a b a b c d c d* rhyme scheme, the metaphysical poem tells of a dream of the persona in which he is brought to judgment by God, who insists: "O man! Confess thy faith! / The word thou speakest saves or bars, / For here are gallows of thy death!" (*MSD*, 3). The persona, however, cannot confess to a faith that is not within him. Instead he defies the Deity:

"Thou art not Him I know! Thou hast / No part in all my vision. Thou / Art Dissonance and Hatred" (*MSD*, 16). The persona chooses this world for his existence, where a love of harmony is the guiding light:

> This life again
> I shall not live, and I would have
> My living soul in flower with love
> Of harmony—that so my death
> Shall be no fall."
>
> (*MSD*, 15)

The poem is filled with a love of life. The persona knows "the stealing beauty of this earth" (*MSD*, 5), remembering that once "I saw my love with tender eyes, / And unbound hair, and girdle free" (*MSD*, 5). The persona realizes that to know beauty and harmony is the "mystery unsealed!" (*MSD*, 18).

Ada Galsworthy omitted "The Dream" from *The Collected Poems of John Galsworthy*, which she compiled and edited in 1934. Apparently she objected to the clearly expressed agnosticism. It was not in keeping with the image of her late husband that she was sculpting. In doing so, she left out Galsworthy's finest poem, his wrestling match with God, equivalent in sincerity, if not in skill and power, to Alfred Tennyson's *In Memoriam* and John Masefield's later *The Everlasting Mercy*.

Galsworthy could also write short, exquisite love lyrics like "Promenade":

> All sweet and startled gravity
> My love comes walking from the Park;
> Her eyes are full of what they've seen—
> The little bushes puffing green,
> The candles pale that light the chestnut tree.
> . . . .
> In dainty shoes and subtle hose
> My love comes walking from the Park.
> She is, I swear, the sweetest thing
> That ever left the heart of Spring,
> To tell the secret: Whence the pollen blows!
>
> (*MSD*, 94)

Few women have ever been so finely portrayed or so subtly glorified
as Goddess of Spring.

Verses New and Old **(1926).**   *Verses New and Old* are mostly old;
that is, almost all of the pieces are reprints or rewrites of poems in
Moods, Songs, and *Doggerels.* New are the 1914–18 poems that at first
reflect Galsworthy's initial patriotic fervor, a fervor shared by most
Europeans in the war's beginning, but one that soon waned for the
author and was replaced by disbelief, horror, and an anger towards a
deity that could allow such slaughter.

In "Valley of the Shadow," a soldier sailing for France prays that
his death, which would be "such a waste of me,"[4] might at least bring
"peace o'er the valleys and cold hills for ever!" (V, 43).

The six quatrains of "The Bells of Peace" are an in memoriam to
the war dead:

> And do they hear, who in their Springtime went?
> The Young, the brave, leaving all behind,
> . . . .
> Leaving the quiet trees and cattle red,
> The southern soft mist over granite tor—
> Whispered from home, by secret valour led
> To face the horror that their souls abhor.
>
> (V, 52)

The church bells demand remembrance, and the persona pleads:
"Ring out the Past, and let not Hate bereave / Our dreaming Dead
of all they died to win!" (V, 53).

The poem is sadly prophetic. Hate did indeed make vain the terrible sacrifices of the war to end all wars.

"Picardy" is a short poem describing that part of France on which
the British Expeditionary Force fought, bled, and died. "Youth's
Own" presents in regular, pedestrian verse a civilian's view of the loss
of life in the war. It contains the most obvious and trite lines in Galsworthy's verse: "Since Youth has vanished from our eyes / Who, living, glad can be?" (V, 47).

Expressing his ambivalence toward God in "Unknown," Galsworthy addresses him as "Lord of cruel happiness" and argues that the
Deity created humankind upon awakening from an unfinished dream,
as an afterthought: "And lo!—this playboy, Man, was born!" (V, 51).

Galsworthy's war poetry, sincere though it is, suffers from his being removed from the direct experience of conflict. They are much

like thousands of competent poems written during the First World War and now forgotten. In no way does his war poetry begin to approach the power of expression of such World War I soldier-poets as Robert Graves, Sigfried Sasoon, and Isaac Rosenberg.

One additional new poem in *Verses New and Old* deserves special mention. The book opens with an eight-line poem for Ada, entitled "Dedication." And despite the fact that without mentioning her name it praises her beauty, the poem is rather a mixed compliment, as the persona compares his lover to a flower that knows "the oldest secret of the world: / How to be loved and still to keep apart" (*V, XI*). But Ada clearly admired the poem, for she retained it in *Collected Poems*.

Collected Poems (1934). Ada Galsworthy, as her late husband's literary executor, gathered together in several volumes fragments of fiction, long-out-of-print stories, unpublished essays, letters, and other pieces, as she attempted to tidy up the Galsworthy canon. *Collected Poems* is one of the more significant results of her efforts. She organized the poems she selected into seven sections: the first, untitled, contains ten early poems, including "Dedication"; the second, titled "Devon and Other Songs for Music," contains most of the songs from *Moods, Songs, and Doggerels;* the third, "In Time of War," comprises the 1914–18 poems from *Verses New and Old;* the fourth, "Frivols," contains short light verse, as if to show that Galsworthy had a light and humorous side, but the only truly amusing piece is entitled "On Accidental Exchange of Opera Hats with John Masefield"; the fifth, "For Love of Beasts," is a collection of animal poems, including "To My Dog" from *Moods, Songs and Doggerels;* the sixth, "Impressions," includes many poems from *Verses New and Old* and several new travel poems, such as "Sweet Oath in Mallorca" and "The Pass of the Song (Arizona)"; the seventh, "The Endless Dream," contains, for the most part, previously uncollected nature poems and poems about dying.[5]

The most noteworthy of the newer works in *Collected Poems* are those in the final section. In "Praised Be the Sun!" Galsworthy speaks of his great love for sunshine that can "warm to substance all that shadows by" (*C*, 125). In the final couplet of the sixteen-line poem he asks that the sun cover him at death: "Praising I live, and when I foundered be, / O thou beloved Sunlight, cover me!" (*C*, 125).

In "So Might It Be!" Galsworthy again hopes for the sun's company at the hour of his death:

Death, when you come to me, let there be sunlight,
Dogs and dear creatures about me at play,
Flowers in the fields and the song of the blackbird—
Spring in the world when you fetch me away!
(C, 131)

At the moment of John Galsworthy's death the sun temporarily broke
through a January fog.[6]

"Bury Hill" is a sonnet of homage to the lovely countryside where
he spent many of his last days and where his ashes were scattered at
his request. In the couplet, speaking both of the end of a day and the
end of his life, he affirmed his oneness with nature: "Here I, too,
stand until the light is gone, / And feed my wonder, while the sheep
graze on!" (C, 130).

The final poem in *Collected Poems*, "Amberley Wildbrooks," named
for an expanse he could see from his windows at Bury House, sums
up Galsworthy's ultimate pantheistic view of life:

Man is a dreamer, waking for a day
. . . .
And momentary dreaming comfort him;
For so he learns, before the long sleep comes,
That in himself revolves the starry scheme,
In him the winter's mute, the summer hums,
Just as it will be in an endless dream.
(CP, 136–37)

Galsworthy did not make a significant contribution to English poetry. He never escaped from Victorian and Edwardian conventions of
subject matter and structure, except in one poem, "To Beauty." He
never experimented with free verse. He was unaffected by the symbol-
ist movement or the later imagists. His own imagery is pedestrian,
and he never connected to myth, as did Yeats, or to the common
man's energy, as did Masefield. Except for "The Dream," only a few
of his short lyrics are memorable. Galsworthy's poetry is worth studying, however, for the direct insight it provides into both his state of
mind at various periods and the way his philosophy developed and
influenced his other writing.

Essays

Despite his enormous output of fiction and drama, John Galsworthy also found time to be a prolific essayist, critic, lecturer, and po-

lemicist. He wrote on subjects as diverse as the creation of character in literature and the contribution of Joseph Conrad to letters; the abuse of women in sweatshops and the slaughtering of animals; and almost any subject imaginable in between. He was quick to take up a cause, and he was not loath to write about his art, although he did so humbly and with the caveat that he was an artist, not a trained critic. Galsworthy's major collections of essays and commentaries are *The Inn of Tranquility* (1912), *A Sheaf* (1916), *Another Sheaf* (1919), *Castles in Spain* (1927), and *Candelabra* (1933).

The Inn of Tranquility. Named after the title piece, itself taken from the name of an inn the Galsworthys visited in Italy, *The Inn of Tranquility* is divided into two parts. The first, "Concerning Life," is a collection of almost storylike recollections of people and experiences: a "new" Italian who finds peaceful, natural vistas too quiet; a bootmaker who starves to death because he refuses to compromise on quality; a dream "allegory of sacred and profane love" (*IT,* 32); a strike by poor women workers in the Midlands who are a "sudden vision of the wild goodness native in humble hearts" (*IT,* 60); a murder of a lost dog (remembering his dog Chris); a family failure; a summon to serve on a grand jury; and a visit to an old slave pen in New Orleans where "the drip, drip, drip of water down the walls was as the sound of a spirit grieving" (*IT,* 131).

The second part of *The Inn of Tranquility,* entitled "Concerning Letters," contains eight essays on the writer's craft. They represent the first significant body of aesthetic commentary by Galsworthy. In "A Novelist's Allegory," an old man serves his community by holding up a light in the night. Bringing light to the dark, the writer's function, is a seemingly trivial, but in fact, vital, function. When the old man dies, the prince says: "Farewell, old man! The Lanthorn is still alight" (*IT,* 188). Then he commands: "Go fetch me another one, and let him carry it!" (*IT,* 188). The light of truth must not, and will not, be extinguished.

"Some Platitudes Concerning Drama" provides an excellent insight into Galsworthy's concepts and techniques as a playwright. He proposes that "the business of the dramatist is so to pose the group as to bring [a] moral poignantly to the light of day" (*IT,* 189). The dramatist has three possible courses: to reflect the codes of life by which the audience lives, a course that ensures popularity; to set his own values before the public and spoon-feed them; or to present life as it really is, doing so with moral detachment. His argument is, of course, for naturalism in theater.

Galsworthy also states that dramatic writing requires a passion for discipline and a determination to be satisfied only with one's finest effort. These qualities then must be applied to the creation of character, for "a human being is the best plot there is" (*IT,* 193).

"Meditation on Finality," "Wanted—Schooling," "Reflections," and "The Windlestraw" criticize through literary example and allegory the public penchant for the trite, the commonplace, and the mediocre. "About Censorship," written in 1909, was part of a crusade Galsworthy was asked to lead by his fellow dramatists against the formal governmental censorship that inhibited the British theater at that time. Satirically, he argues that if censorship is good and necessary for the theater, it is equally good and necessary for literature, art, science, medicine, and, of course, politics.

Finally, in a Tolstoy-like essay, "Vague Thoughts on Art," Galsworthy addresses the old aesthetic question: what is art? Galsworthy's personal aesthetic is clear: "Art is that imaginative expression of human energy, which, through technical concretion of feeling and perception, tends to reconcile the individual with the universal, by exciting in him impersonal emotions" (*IT,* 255). By impersonal emotions Galsworthy means objectivity; the artist's creativity leads him to a depersonalized oneness with the archetypical human experience.

A Sheaf (1916).   Galsworthy dedicated *A Sheaf* to the drama critic William Archer. He called the collection of "non-creative writings" the "wild oats of a novelist, which the writer has been asked to bind up."[7] Forty essays are divided among these categories: "On the Treatment of Animals," "Concerning Laws," "On Prisons and Punishments," "On the Position of Women," "On Social Unrest," "On Peace," "The War," "And—After?" Finally, in a category by itself, there is a patriotic 1916 speech, "The Islands of the Blessed," in which he prophetically calls for nations to seize the opportunity to set up "a Court of Nations, backed this time by real force," in the hope of preventing another world war (*S,* 384).

A Sheaf addresses most of the social values Galsworthy supported throughout his life, as well as his antiwar and antihate bias. Reading this book today reminds the contemporary reader of how the more enlightened of Galsworthy's generation struggled to bring about the social advances all accept with little thought today, including: laws for humane slaughter of animals, child labor laws, fairer divorce laws, woman's suffrage, humane prison conditions, and others. He also discusses the changing British Empire, the effect of the war on art and literature, and the possible change the first national conscription might have on Britain. One essay, "A Last Word," demands that postwar Britain "begin at once transmuting into deeds those words: Freedom, Health, Justice, for all" (*S,* 367). Galsworthy realized before the war ended that Britain had to move down the road to socialism and equality if the sacrifices of the people were to have any long-term meaning.

Another Sheaf (1919). *Another Sheaf* contains eleven essays and one futuristic allegory, "Grotesques," about an angel visiting Britain in 1947, thirty years in the future for Galsworthy, and thirty years after what the angel and his interpreter call The Great Skirmish. Alas, the angel learns that "there is no poetry now."[8] The nation has failed to take advantage of the possibilities of change created by the war and has not turned to simpler living by decreasing need, eating plainer food, using preventative medicine, and generally doing what is now called down-scaling. Instead, the interpreter, called the dragoman, tells the angel, "Wealthy again we may be; healthy and happy we are not, as yet" (*AS,* 261).

The essays in *Another Sheaf* deal with such subjects as comparisons of different national characters, land use and agricultural reform in a nation that clearly needed to grow more food, impressions of France during the war, and the drama in England and America. This last piece, though somewhat out-of-place, is the one work of lasting interest in the book. In it Galsworthy decries the reluctance of actor-managers to mount the new plays of Shaw, Barrie, John Millington Synge, and, of course, Galsworthy, because of their pandering to popular taste and their fear of the new, despite support from the drama critics. The author argues that producers need to realize that the theater audience is irrevocably split into two groups, one large and one much smaller, the latter willing to support the intellectual and artistic innovations of the avant-garde. Finally, Galsworthy predicts that "dramatic art, which of all is most dependent on a favourable economic condition, will gravitate towards America, which may well become in the next ten years not only the mother, but the foster-mother of the best Anglo-Saxon drama" (*AS,* 105).

Castles in Spain (1927). *Castles in Spain* contains fourteen pieces, several of which were originally prefaces or addresses. The title piece, an address, asks: "Of what do moderns dream? What are our castles in Spain?[9] The dream he would wish moderns to embrace is one centering on "the sense of human dignity, which is but a love of and a belief in beauty" (*CS*, 22). In "Where We Stand," Galsworthy argues against coal as a fuel and export and supports water power for electrification. Once more he advocates British self-sufficiency in food production. "International Thought," written in 1923, warns of the danger of destructive science.

The literary pieces in *Castles in Spain* are the most enduring, adding to Galsworthy's aesthetic, and offering his evaluation of some of his contemporaries. "On Expression" praises novelists whose characters are inhabited by a "familiar spirit," which convinces the reader "that he might meet and recognize them walking the every-day world" (*CS*, 65). Praising Tolstoy as well as fellow English writers Hardy, Bennett, and Wells, Galsworthy concludes that "the perfect example of "familiar spirit" permeating both book and its characters is in Mark Twain's *Huckleberry Finn*" (*CS*, 67). "Reminiscences of Conrad" relates Galsworthy's long acquaintance with the sailor-writer he first met on the clipper *Torrens* in March 1893. Galsworthy describes his friend's work habits and his personal traits. He also offers brief evaluations of Conrad's novels and finally praises him as a writer who "worked in the sweat of spirit and body" (*CS*, 125). "Preface to Conrad's Plays" gently concludes that it was a good thing Conrad devoted little time to drama. "Foreword to *Green Mansions*" praises W. H. Hudson as an inheritor of Tolstoy's skill and values.

Written in 1903, "After Seeing a Play" predates Galsworthy's debut as a dramatist. It is especially interesting because it documents the author's dissatisfaction with the "old" drama's obsession with position and marriage. He argues for concentration on "love and death." For him, "art is rooted in feeling . . . [and] the only epic virtue is courage" (*CS*, 200). Yet when Galsworthy commenced play writing, position and marriage became central to his dramaturgy, and great courage would seldom be an attribute of his protagonists.

"Six Novelists in Profile" discusses those novelists Galsworthy considered great humanists: Dickens, Turgenev, de Maupassant, Tolstoy, Conrad, and Anatole France. "Books as Ambassadors" is cynical of their service: "Books will be Books! Peace-making or belligerent, like men" (*CS*, 243).

The last and most significant essay in *Castles in Spain* is "Faith of a Novelist," in which he states: "Truth and beauty are a hard quest, but what else is there worth seeking?" (*CS*, 262). The reward of a novelist is "unconsciousness of self," for he cannot conceive a "First Cause." It is better to work than dwell on beginning and ends. Life is always a mystery and must not only be accepted as it is, but also loved. As to critics, he asks that they "should always be ready to accept the theme and the medium selected by the artist, and having accepted, should then criticize the work for being, or not being, what it is meant to be" (*CS*, 261).

Candelabra (1933). *Candelabra* is primarily a reissue of selections from *The Inn of Tranquility, Another Sheaf,* and *Castles in Spain.* New are three addresses delivered between 1928 and 1931. The first, "Four More Novelists in Profile," documents Galsworthy's admiration for Alexandre Dumas père, Anton Chekhov, Robert Louis Stevenson, and his old friend W. H. Hudson, who surely does not belong in the same classification with the others. "Literature and Life" proposes that good literature contains "vitality in . . . characters" and "must have genuine individuality of its own. It must be essentially unlike what has gone before."[10] The link between literature and life is verisimilitude in characterization, for quality literature only "comes into being . . . when Life strikes sparks out of a temperament" (*CA*, 275). The good writer becomes totally involved in his creation, knowing that "to forget self is the key to happiness" (*CA*, 282).

In "The Creation of Character in Literature," Galsworthy, after a lifetime of writing, concludes that such creation is a mystery that cannot be defined or documented. He concludes that Shakespeare was the world's greatest creator of living characters because, seemingly, he understood intuitively that people deeply crave to see themselves, their loves ones, their friends, and their enemies portrayed as types and reconstituted in a fiction. Moreover, "the enduring characters in literature are ever such as have kicked free of swaddling clothes and their creators. . . . You may see their stars and share their troubles, laugh with them, love with them, draw the breath of their defiances, suffer in their struggles, float out with them into the unconscious when their night comes" (*CA*, 311). As he spoke these words in 1931, Galsworthy surely thought of his most enduring character: Soames Forsyte.

Galsworthy's essays, like his poetry, help the reader to understand the scope of his interests and the nature of his genius. In what he called his noncreative work, one learns of the causes and movements dear to his heart, which he also addressed more subtly in his "creative" work. The essays also inform us of his personal aesthetic, his thoughts about deity, and the qualities he admired in other writers. Last, they show us a gentle, tolerant, peace-loving, compassionate human being.

Chapter Nine
Achievement and Summation

During the last ten years of his life, Galsworthy's reputation was greater than his talent. Fifty-odd years after his death it is apparent that his talent is greater than his reputation. He had been quickly dismissed, partly in reaction to the overpraise he had received, partly because he was deemed by some critics to be a sociological writer and reformer whose causes came one by one to fulfillment, partly because his range seemed limited to the upper-middle-class and upper-class world with which he was most familiar, and partly because his technique as a fiction writer, if not as a playwright, was old-fashioned. Surely he did not concern himself much with the problems of form, and thus he was able to slip back and forth from novel to story. He was concerned with truth, and he admirably expressed that truth he saw and understood. If he did so in conventional ways, and if simultaneously he espoused humanitarianism, idealism, tolerance, human dignity, and the code of a gentleman, he was not the lesser artist for it. In that he could see and express universal and archetypal patterns in the common experiences of his youth and maturity, he was a great writer.

Growth and Development

Success came slowly to Galsworthy. He was thirty by the time his first book was published. That work and his second he published at his own cost. At thirty-five he had spent more money on his writing than he had received in payment. It was only in 1906, with the publication of *A Man of Property* and the production of *The Silver Box,* that serious critical recognition and financial success came his way. By that time he had taught himself—through constant practice, by listening to knowledgeable critics and writers, and by studying Turgenev—to observe carefully and write precisely about three topics: tragic love in conflict with unbending society, the British class system, and the complicated codes of social behavior. He also learned to express deep emotion and love of beauty without sacrificing verisimilitude.

At the beginning of his career, after intitial experimentation, Galsworthy wrote a series of novels, from *The Island Pharisees* (1904) through *The Freelands* (1915), that excoriate upper-middle-class British society. Always, however, there is a passionate love affair at the core of a Galsworthy story. Frequently it is one involving an unhappily married lover, but Galsworthy never attacks marriage as an institution—only individual marriages without love.

When the First World War approached, Galsworthy realized that the society he knew and wrote about would change irrevocably, and so he turned to novels of romance in which he could fully explore passionate, but unapproved, relationships between men and women. These novels failed, and he found his hard-earned reputation as a novelist atrophying. At the war's end he realized that his strength was in his ability to chronicle the great British upper middle class, which had just passed from power, and so he returned to his favorite literary family, the Forsytes, and his favorite period, the late Victorian–Edwardian era, and finished the *Saga,* jumping over the abhorred war in the process. It made him world famous in 1922, and so he continued "The Forsyte Chronicles" with another trilogy, *A Modern Comedy* (1929). Having finally killed off his great upper-middle-class protagonist, Soames Forsyte, at the end of *A Modern Comedy,* he spent the rest of his life chronicling an upper-class family of the landed gentry, the Charwells, in the trilogy *End of the Chapter* (1934).

As a dramatist he was one of those playwrights, including Shaw, Barrie, and Granville-Barker, who rejuvenated English drama. He quickly, seemingly almost effortlessly, adopted Ibsenite realism and French naturalism to his own secular humanism, producing a powerful drama that replaced fiction for him as his medium of protest and reform. His pre–World War I plays indict British social institutions and the hypocrisy of the privileged classes. He also attacks the intolerance, selfishness, and lack of compassion of his fellow humans. After the war, he continued these themes, subtly mellowing and becoming more accepting of human inadequacies. His finest plays—*Strife* (1909), *Justice* (1910), *The Skin Game* (1920), and *Loyalties* (1922)—successfully combine ethical themes, naturalistic dramaturgy, powerful characterization, and authentic dialogue.

His friend Ford Madox (Hueffer) Ford summed up Galsworthy's contribution to the theater: "No other modern dramatist has anything approaching Galsworthy's loftiness of mind, his compassion, his poetry, his occasional sunlight or the instinctive knowledge of what you can do on the stage. And by himself he lifted the modern stage to a plane until his time it had seemed impossible that it could attain."[1]

Galsworthy's stories, particularly *Five Tales* (1918), show great mastery of the form, again using straightforward narrative in a noncontroversial way. "The Apple Tree" and the interlude "Indian Summer of a Forsyte," from *Five Tales,* are his outstanding contributions to the genre.

Achievement

"The Forsyte Chronicles" is the most authentic literary portrait of Britain's great Edwardian upper middle class. It is the recognized English national family epic, embodying all the virtues and vices a people chose to see in themselves: integrity, endurance, respect for tradition, love of fair play, courage, dedication to justice, and respect for women; but also reserve, snobbery, class rigidity, conventionality, and noncommunicativeness. The chronicles achieved a lasting readership in Galsworthy's lifetime, and they have sustained a large and appreciative audience through the nadir years of Galsworthy critical appreciation. That audience read the fall of the Forsyte nation as an allegory for the fall of their own. Additionally, for much of the world, from New Delhi to Moscow, Galsworthy's portrait of the English confirmed and concretized the perceptions of millions. The writing of the chronicles may prove to be the most significant literary production of its time.

In addition, his plays helped change the justice system, brought about some prison reform, somewhat alleviated labor-management and middle-class—upper-class strains, eased the plight of poor women, and pointed out anti-Semitism in British society long before it was fashionable to do so. A political party leader would be proud to have had the impact Galsworthy had on his era, a time when an important writer was a spokesperson listened to and respected.

Influence

Since it quickly became fashionable to discount Galsworthy as the "bourgeois master," few writers coming after him admitted to his influence, although it is inconceivable that a British writer born at the turn of the century or later would not have read his work. It is clear, however, that the post–World War I generation of novelists owed much to Galsworthy. Aldous Huxley's pre–World War II novels, particularly *Point Counter Point* (1928), *Eyeless in Gaza* (1936), and *After Many a Summer Dies the Swan* (1939), share the sense of beleaguered and perplexed liberalism that Galsworthy evidenced in the social novels, and even the dystopian *Brave New World* (1932) evolves from the Edwardian concern for the society of the future most acutely articulated by Galsworthy and H. G. Wells.

Evelyn Waugh's perennial theme of the destructiveness in and of upper-class society, best illustrated in *Brideshead Revisited* (1945), also derives from Galsworthy's satiric treatment of that class, not only in the social novels but in the chronicles. C. P. Snow's protagonist, Lewis Eliot, in the eleven-novel saga *Strangers and Brothers* (1940–70), with his miserable marriage and generally thwarted life, recalls the ever evolving, often perplexed Soames Forsyte, and Snow's use of contemporary events as backdrop to his social novels directly derives from Galsworthy's technique in *A Modern Comedy* and *End of the Chapter*. Last, the desire for a more just society expressed in the novels of the Angry Young Men, particularly John Braine's *Room at the Top* (1957), evolves from the social criticism found in Galsworthy's early novels, as well as from the fiction of other Edwardians. With the currently renewed critical interest in Galsworthy, another generation of British writers will find many problems and ideas in Galsworthy worth exploring.

In the drama, the work of Britain's post–World War II Angry Young Men, particularly John Osborne's *Look Back in Anger* (1957) and *The Entertainer* (1960), reflects Galsworthy's belief that the theater was the best marketplace for social and political ideas. All contemporary British dramatists, working in naturalistic settings if not with realistic themes, owe a debt to Galsworthy's fastidious devotion to theatrical naturalism. The strident dialogue of *Strife* leads to the unconstrained and free-tongued language of Harold Pinter and Tom Stoppard.

Galsworthy's plays are being revived on the stage and on TV. The social themes of his dramas—women's rights, class conflict, labor-management strife, prison reform, and others—remain current. Directors and actors are finding that he has engrossing plots and vivid characterizations awaiting rediscovery.

Conclusion

A. C. Ward notes that Galsworthy "was moved throughout his life by an acute sense of social justice, and though he aimed to hold the balance fairly between rich and poor, between the powerful and the helpless, his emotions were always engaged on the side of the underdog."[2] This is the centrist position—in politics, in social philosophy, in economics. Galsworthy's work is at the heart of British social values as well as English literary tradition. The line of humanist social novelists from Fielding to Dickens and Thackeray to Hardy passes through Galsworthy on to C. P. Snow and the future.

In "Four More Novelists in Profile" Galsworthy says, "The unseen motion of Time's fan drifts to the winds all that has not the magic stuff 'life' in it" (*CA*, 269). Galsworthy's work once drifted to the winds. It has drifted back. The magic stuff is there after all.

Notes and References

Chapter One

1. David Holloway, *John Galsworthy* (London: Morgan—Grampian, 1969), 78.
2. Catherine Dupré, *John Galsworthy* (New York: Coward, McGann & Geoghegan, 1976), 12.
3. H. V. Marrot, *The Life and Letters of John Galsworthy* (New York: Scribner's, 1936), 25.
4. Dupré, *Galsworthy,* 16.
5. M. E. Reynolds, *Memories of John Galsworthy* (London: Robert Hale, 1936), 15.
6. Ibid., 17.
7. R. H. Mottram, *For Some We Loved* (London: Hutchinson, 1956), 33.
8. As quoted in Marrot, *Life and Letters,* 109.
9. Dudley Barker, *The Man of Principle* (London: George Allen & Unwin, 1963), 26–27.
10. Edward Garnett, *Letters from John Galsworthy 1900–1932* (London: Jonathan Cape, 1934), 133–44.
11. Rudolph Sauter, *Galsworthy the Man* (London: Peter Owen, 1967), 122.
12. Marrot, *Life and Letters,* 33.
13. As quoted in Barker, *Man of Principle,* 30.
14. Ibid.
15. As quoted in Marrot, *Life and Letters,* 66.
16. Ibid., 70.
17. Dupré, *Galsworthy,* 50–51.
18. Ibid., 51.
19. Barker, *Man of Principle,* 52–53.
20. As quoted in Dupré, *Galsworthy,* 48.
21. Marrot, *Life and Letters,* 101.
22. Dupré, *Galsworthy,* 54.
23. Ada Galsworthy, *Over the Hills and Far Away* (London: Robert Hale, 1937), 9.
24. Mottram, *For Some,* 32.
25. As quoted in Dupré, *Galsworthy,* 65.
26. Garnett, *Letters,* 5.
27. Mottram, *For Some,* 22.
28. Ibid., 74.

29. Barker, *Man of Principle*, 200.

30. Ada Galsworthy, *Our Dear Dogs* (New York: Scribner's, 1953), 16.

31. Garnett, *Letters*, 68–69.

32. Ibid., 91.

33. Barker, *Man of Principle*, 117.

34. First production dates given for plays.

35. Barker, *Man of Principle*, 22.

36. Ibid., 52.

37. Garnett, *Letters*, 127.

38. Margaret Morris, *My Galsworthy Story* (London: Peter Owen, 1967), 21.

39. Ibid., 23.

40. Ibid., 54.

41. Ibid., 126.

42. Ibid., 124.

43. Ada Galsworthy, *Over the Hills*, 99.

44. Ibid., 255.

45. Ibid., 228.

46. Barker, *Man of Principle*, 174.

47. Dupré, *Galsworthy*, 232.

48. Garnett, *Letters*, 218.

49. Barker, *Man of Principle*, 184.

50. Hermon Ould, *John Galsworthy* (London: Chapman & Hall, 1934), 74–75.

51. Holloway, *Galsworthy*, 38, 40.

52. As quoted in Dupré, *Galsworthy*, 279.

53. R. H. Mottram, *John Galsworthy* (London: Longmans, Green, 1953), 32–33.

54. As quoted in Dupré, *Galsworthy*, 287.

Chapter Two

1. Virginia Woolf, "Mr. Bennett and Mrs. Brown," in *Approaches to the Novel*, ed. Robert Scholes (San Francisco: Chandler, 1961), 219.

2. Ibid.

3. John Batchelor, *The Edwardian Novelists* (New York: St. Martin's, 1982), 26.

4. Dupré, *Galsworthy*, 57.

5. *Jocelyn* (London: Duckworth, 1898; reprint, London: Sidgwick & Jackson, 1976), 80.

6. Dupré, *Galsworthy*, 67.

7. Ibid.

8. *Villa Rubein*, rev. ed. (New York: Putnam, 1908), 20.

9. See William Bellamy, *The Novels of Wells, Bennett, and Galsworthy: 1890–1910* (New York: Barnes & Noble, 1971), 11–13.

10. As quoted in Marrot, *Life and Letters,* 54.

11. Ibid.

12. Ibid.

13. Alec Fréchet, *John Galsworthy: A Reassessment* (Totowa, N.J.: Barnes & Noble, 1982), 64.

14. *The Island Pharisees,* rev. ed. (New York: Scribner's, 1920), 9; hereafter cited in the text as *IP*.

15. Vida Marković, *The Reputation of Galsworthy in England, 1897–1950* (Belgrade: University of Belgrade Press, 1968), 51–53.

16. Garnett, *Letters,* 12.

17. Bellamy, *Wells, Bennett, and Galsworthy,* 183.

18. Ibid., 180.

19. *The Country House* (New York: Putnam, 1908), 305; hereafter cited in the text as *CH*.

20. *Fraternity* (London: Heinemann, 1909), 149; hereafter cited in the text as *F*.

21. Edward Wagenknecht, *Cavalcade of the English Novel* (New York: Holt, 1943), 492.

22. Leon Schalit, *John Galsworthy: A Survey* (London: Heinemann, 1929), 135.

23. D. H. Lawrence, "John Galsworthy," in *Scrutinies,* ed. Edgell Rickword (London: Wishart, 1928), 69.

24. As quoted in Marrot, *Life and Letters,* 285.

25. Sanford Sternlicht, *John Masefield* (Boston: Twayne, 1977), 81–82.

26. William C. Frierson, *The English Novel in Transition, 1885–1940* (Norman: University of Oklahoma, 1942; reprint, New York: Cooper Square, 1965), 131.

27. *The Patrician* (New York: Scribner's, 1913), 137; hereafter cited in the text as *P*.

28. *The Freelands* (London: Heinemann, 1915), 3; hereafter cited in the text as *FR*.

29. Fréchet, *A Reassessment,* 81–82.

30. *The Dark Flower* (London: Heinemann, 1913), 301; hereafter cited in the text as *DF*.

31. Marrot, *Life and Letters,* 377.

32. *Beyond* (London: Heinemann, 1917), 420–21.

33. Mottram, *For Some,* 166.

34. *Saint's Progress* (London: Heinemann, 1919), 402–3.

35. Schalit, *A Survey,* 186.

36. *The Burning Spear* (London: Chatto & Windus: 1919), 224.

37. Frierson, *Novel in Transition,* 162.

Chapter Three

1. *A Modern Comedy* (New York: Scribner's, 1930), v.

2. *The Man of Property* (London: Heinemann, 1906), 4; hereafter cited in the text as *MP*.

3. *The Works of John Galsworthy,* Manaton Edition (London: Heinemann, 1923–36), 7:xi.

4. Denis de Rougemont, *Love in the Western World,* rev. ed. (New York: Doubleday, 1956), 288.

5. "Indian Summer of a Forsyte," in *Five Tales* (London: Heinemann, 1918), 297.

6. *In Chancery,* in *The Forsyte Saga* (London: Heinemann, 1922), 733–34; hereafter cited in the text as *IC*.

7. *Awakening* (London: Heinemann, 1920), 11; hereafter cited in the text as *A*.

8. *To Let,* in *The Forsyte Saga,* 805–6; hereafter cited in the text as *TL*.

9. André Chevrillon, *Three Studies in English Literature: Kipling, Galsworthy, Shakespeare* (1923; reprint, Port Washington, N.Y.: Kennikat, 1967), 162.

Chapter Four

1. Barker, *Man of Principle,* 206.

2. *The White Monkey,* in *A Modern Comedy,* 7; hereafter cited in the text as *WM*.

3. *The Silver Spoon,* in *A Modern Comedy,* 504.

4. "Passers By" in *A Modern Comedy,* 507; hereafter cited in the text as *PB*.

5. *Swan Song,* in *A Modern Comedy,* 537; hereafter cited in the text as *SS*.

6. *A Modern Comedy,* x.

7. "Soames and the Flag," in *On Forsyte 'Change* (New York: Scribner's, 1930), 277.

Chapter Five

1. Mottram, *For Some,* 269.

2. Marrot, *Life and Letters,* 629.

3. *Maid in Waiting,* in *End of the Chapter* (New York: Scribner's, 1934), 12; hereafter cited in the text as *MW*.

4. *Flowering Wilderness,* in *End of the Chapter,* 393; hereafter cited in the text as *FW*.

5. *Over the River,* in *End of the Chapter,* 604; hereafter cited in the text as *OR*.

Chapter Six

1. As quoted in Schalit, *A Survey,* 178.
2. Ibid.
3. As quoted in Mottram, *For Some,* 41.
4. *A Man of Devon* (London: Blackwood, 1901), 185; hereafter cited in the text as *MD.*
5. *A Commentary* (London: Grant Richards, 1908), 49; herafter cited in the text as *C.*
6. *A Motley* (New York: Scribner's, 1914), 6; hereafter cited in the text as *M.*
7. *The Little Man and Other Satires* (New York: Scribner's, 1915), 276.
8. Dupré, *Galsworthy,* 222.
9. *Five Tales,* 256; hereafter cited in the text as *FT.*
10. See Eugene E. Zumwalt, "The Myth of the Garden in Galsworthy's 'The Apple Tree,' " *Research Studies of the State College of Washington* XXVII (September 1959):129–34.
11. *Tatterdemalion* (New York: Scribner's, 1920), 25; hereafter cited in the text as *T.*
12. *Captures* (New York: Scribner's, 1923), 52; hereafter cited in the text as *CAP.*
13. Joseph J. Reilly, "John Galsworthy and His Short Stories," *The Catholic World* 123 (1926):761.

Chapter Seven

1. First production dates given for plays.
2. William Archer, *The Old Drama and the New* (Boston: Small, Maynard, 1923), 364.
3. Ford Madox (Hueffer) Ford, "Galsworthy," in *Portraits from Life* (New York: Houghton, 1937), 139.
4. John Gassner, *Masters of the Drama* (New York: Dover, 1954), 616.
5. Asher Boldon Wilson, *John Galsworthy's Letters to Leon Lion* (The Hague: Mouton, 1968), 56.
6. Marrot, *Life and Letters,* 189.
7. *The Plays of John Galsworthy* (New York: Scribner's, 1928), 32; hereafter cited in the text as *PL.*
8. R. H. Coates, *John Galsworthy as Dramatic Artist* (London: Duckworth, 1926), 177.
9. *The Inn of Tranquility* (New York: Scribner's, 1912), 192–93; hereafter cited in the text as *IT.*
10. William York Tyndall, *Forces in Modern British Literature* (New York: Vintage, 1956), 41.
11. Mottram, *For Some,* 127.

12. Marrot, *Life and Letters,* 330.

13. V. Dupont, *John Galsworthy: The Dramatic Artist* (Paris: Didier, 1942), 51.

14. Schalit, *A Survey,* 255.

15. Mottram, *For Some,* 137.

16. Schalit, *A Survey,* 303.

17. Dupré, *Galsworthy,* 273.

18. Mottram, *For Some, Galsworthy,* 276.

19. James Gindin, *The English Climate* (Ann Arbor: Michigan University Press, 1979), 212. Ada Galsworthy published the fragment in *Forsytes, Pendyces, and Others* (New York: Scribner's, 1935), 247–87.

20. *The Works of John Galsworthy,* 18:x.

Chapter Eight

1. Mottram, *For Some,* 57.

2. *Moods, Songs, and Doggerals* (New York: Scribner's, 1912), 97; hereafter cited in the text as *MSD.*

3. Garnett, *Letters,* 30.

4. *Verses Old and New* (London: Heinemann, 1926), 43; hereafter cited in the text as *V.*

5. *The Collected Poems of John Galsworthy* (London: Heinemann, 1934), 84; hereafter cited in the text as *C.*

6. Barker, *Man of Principle,* 235.

7. *A Sheaf* (New York: Scribner's, 1916), vii; hereafter cited in the text as *S.*

8. *Another Sheaf* (London: Heinemann, 1919), 205; hereafter cited in the text as *AS.*

9. *Castles in Spain* (New York: Scribner's, 1927), 3; hereafter cited in the text as *CS.*

10. *Candelabra* (New York: Scribner's, 1933), 274; hereafter cited in the text as *CA.*

Chapter Nine

1. Ford, "Galsworthy," 140.

2. A. C. Ward, *Longman Companion to Twentieth Century Literature* (London: Longman, 1970), 219.

Selected Bibliography

PRIMARY SOURCES

1. Collected Editions
The Devon Edition of the Novels, Tales, and Plays of John Galsworthy. 22 vols.
New York: Scribner's, 1926–29.
The Manaton Edition of the Works of John Galsworthy. 30 vols. London: Heine-
mann, 1923–36. Most complete edition. Contains prefaces by the au-
thor.

2. Novels

a. Trilogies
The Forsyte Saga. London: Heinemann, 1922.
A Modern Comedy. London: Heinemann, 1929.
End of the Chapter. London: Heinemann, 1935.

b. Separate Works
Beyond. London: Heinemann, 1917.
The Burning Spear. London: Chatto & Windus, 1019. Published as by
"A. R. P——M."
The Country House. London: Heinemann, 1907.
The Dark Flower. London: Heinemann, 1913.
Flowering Wilderness. London: Heinemann, 1932.
Fraternity. London: Heinemann, 1909.
The Freelands. London: Heinemann, 1915.
In Chancery. London: Heinemann, 1920.
The Island Pharisees. London: Heinemann, 1904.
Jocelyn. London: Heinemann, 1904. Published as by "John Sinjohn."
Maid in Waiting. London: Heinemann, 1931.
The Man of Property. London: Heinemann, 1906.
Over the River. London: Heinemann, 1933. American title: *One More River.*
The Patrician. London: Heinemann, 1911.
A Saint's Progress. London: Heinemann, 1919.
The Silver Spoon. London: Heinemann, 1926.
Swan Song. London: Heinemann, 1928.
To Let. London: Heinemann, 1921.
Villa Rubein. London: Duckworth, 1900. Published as by "John Sinjohn."
The White Monkey. London: Heinemann, 1924.

3. Short Stories
Awakening. London: Heinemann, 1920.
Captures. London: Heinemann, 1923.
Caravan. London: Heinemann, 1925.
A Commentary. London: Grant Richards, 1908.
Five Tales. London: Heinemann, 1918.
Forsytes, Pendyces, and Others. London: Heinemann, 1935.
From the Four Winds. London: T. Fisher Unwin, 1897. Published as by "John
     Sinjohn."
The Little Man and Other Satires. London: Heinemann, 1915.
A Man of Devon. London: Blackwood, 1901. Published as by "John Sin-
     john."
A Motley. London: Heinemann, 1910.
On Forsyte 'Change. London: Heinemann, 1930.
Tatterdemalion. London: Heinemann, 1920.
Two Forsyte Interludes. London: Heinemann, 1927.

4. Plays

a. Collected Plays
Plays. London: Duckworth, 1929. Almost all the major plays and six short
     plays.
Plays: The Silver Box, Joy, Strife. London: Duckworth, 1909.
Six Short Plays. London: Duckworth, 1921.

b. Separate Works
A Bit O' Love. London: Duckworth, 1915.
The Eldest Son. London: Duckworth, 1912.
Escape. London: Duckworth, 1926.
Exiled. London: Duckworth, 1929.
A Family Man. London: Duckworth, 1922.
The Forest. London: Duckworth, 1924.
The Foundations. London: Duckworth, 1920.
The Fugitive. London: Duckworth, 1913.
Justice. London: Duckworth, 1910.
The Little Dream. London: Duckworth, 1911.
Loyalties. London: Duckworth, 1922.
The Mob. London: Duckworth, 1914.
Old English. London: Duckworth, 1924.
The Pigeon. London: Duckworth, 1912.
The Roof. London: Duckworth, 1929.
The Show. London: Duckworth, 1925.
The Skin Game. London: Duckworth, 1920.
Windows. London: Duckworth, 1922.
The Winter Garden. London: Duckworth, 1935.

5. Poems
The Collected Poems of John Galsworthy. London: Heinemann, 1934.
Moods, Songs, and Doggerels. London: Heinemann, 1912.
Verses New and Old. London: Heinemann, 1926.

6. Essays
Another Sheaf. London: Heinemann, 1919.
A Sheaf. London: Heinemann, 1916.
Candelabra. London: Heinemann, 1933.
Castles in Spain. London: Heinemann, 1927.
The Inn of Tranquility. London: Heinemann, 1912.

SECONDARY SOURCES

1. Bibliographies
Fabes, Gilbert H. *John Galsworthy, His First Editions.* London: W. and G. Foyle, 1932. Alphabetical. English editions only.
Marrot, H. V. *A Bibliography of the Works of John Galsworthy.* London: Elkin Mathews & Marrot, 1928. Cites English and American first editions of novels, stories, plays, and essays. Also a bibliography of early criticism only through 1928.
Stevens, Earl E., and H. Ray Stevens. *John Galsworthy: An Annotated Bibliography of Writings about Himself.* De Kalb: Northern Illinois University Press, 1980. Worldwide in scope. Excellent annotations. Indispensable research tool.

2. Books
Barker, Dudley. *The Man of Principle.* London: George Allen & Unwin, 1967. Light study of Galsworthy's life and work. Perspective halfway between the idolatry of Marrot and the iconoclasm of Dupré.
Batchelor, John. *The Edwardian Novelists.* New York: St. Martin's, 1982. Useful introduction to the milieu and concerns of major Edwardian novelists. Distances Galsworthy from H. G. Wells and Arnold Bennett.
Bellamy, William. *the Novels of Wells, Bennett, and Galsworthy: 1890–1910.* New York: Barnes & Noble, 1971. Major study of early novels of these writers, rescuing them from thirty years of hostile criticism.
Chevrillon, André. *Three Studies in English Literature: Kipling, Galsworthy, Shakespeare.* 1923. Reprint, Port Washington, N.Y.: Kennikat, 1967. Adulatory study of *The Forsyte Saga.* Insights into psychology of major characters.
Coates, R. H. *John Galsworthy as a Dramatic Artist.* London: Duckworth, 1926. First book-length study of Galsworthy's plays. Thematically organized.

Cross, Wilbur. L. *Four Contemporary Novelists.* New York: Macmillan, 1930. Early prediction of perennial popularity of *The Forsyte Saga* and decline of interest in the other novels.

Dupont, V. *John Galsworthy: The Dramatic Artist.* Paris: Didier, 1942. Survey. Faults the melodrama, praises realism and atmosphere, explains Galsworthy's dramaturgy.

Dupré, Catherine. *John Galsworthy.* New York: Coward, McCann & Geoghegan, 1976. Incisive biography, but too negative in assessment of Galsworthy's contribution to the novel.

Fréchet, Alec. *John Galsworthy: A Reassessment.* Totowa, N.J.: Barnes & Noble, 1982. Sensible overall study. Demonstrates innovative aspects of Galsworthy's art.

Frierson, William C. *The English Novel in Transition,* 1885–1940. Standard study of post-Dickens novel emphasizing role of French naturalism in its development.

Galsworthy, Ada. *Our Dear Dogs.* London: Heinemann, 1935; reprint, London: St. Catherine Press, 1953. Picture catalog of the Galsworthy dogs. Insights into domestic life and passion for animals.

————.*Over the Hills and Far Away.* London: Robert Hale, 1937. Travelogue of places visited by peripatetic Galsworthys. Also relates war experiences in France and fund-raising for war effort.

Garnett, Edward, ed. *Letters from John Galsworthy.* London: Jonathan Cape, 1934. Galsworthy's letters to his early mentor. Also key letters from Garnett to Galsworthy. Shows Garnett's influence on Galsworthy's development.

Gindin, James. *The English Climate: An Excursion into a Biography of John Galsworthy.* Ann Arbor: University of Michigan Press, 1979. Unfocused, self-serving travelogue purporting to show process of researching biography. Interviews with relatives and survivors in 1970s. Galsworthy gossip, anecdotes, and trivia.

Holloway, David. *John Galsworthy.* London: Morgan—Grampian, 1969. Brief but excellent overview and biography.

Marković, Vida. *The Reputation of Galsworthy in England, 1897–1950.* Belgrade: Faculty of Philology of the University of Belgrade Press, 1968. Predicts a return of critical and general interest in Galsworthy. Discusses early reception and later disaffection of critics.

Marrot, H. V. *The Life and Letters of John Galsworthy.* New York: Scribner's, 1936. Indispensable official biography. Alters the facts of premarital relationship between John and Ada.

Morris, Margaret. *My Galsworthy Story.* London: Peter Owen, 1967. Memoir of Galsworthy's one extramarital love affair.

Mottram, R. H. *For Some We Loved.* London: Hutchinson, 1956. Periphrastic hagiography by protégé. Intimate sketches of private life. Discusses Galsworthy's relationships with other writers.

————. *John Galsworthy*. London: Longmans, Green, 1953. Brief, saccharine appreciation.

Ould, Hermon. *John Galsworthy*. London: Chapman & Hall, 1934. Early thematic study by associate in PEN. Refutes D. H. Lawrence's attack on Galsworthy's supposed lack of sexuality.

Reynolds, M. E. *Memories of John Galsworthy*. London: Robert Hale, 1936. Early recollections by an adoring younger sister, and her letters from Galsworthy.

Sauter, Rudolph. *Galsworthy the Man*. London: Peter Owen, 1967. Personal reminiscence by hero-worshiping nephew who lived and traveled with him for eight years.

Schalit, Leon. *John Galsworthy: A Survey*. London: Heinemann, 1929. Accolade at the height of Galsworthy's popularity by his German translator.

Wilson, Asher Boldon. *John Galsworthy's Letters to Leon Lion*. The Hague; Mouton, 1968. Ostensibly the record of relationship between playwright and his producer, but more than one-third deals with Galsworthy's impact on English stage. Excellent introduction to Galsworthy as dramatist.

Index

823.912
G178

119 770

DATE DUE

DEMCO 38-297